"Christmas is such a special time in which we should slow down and ponder the deeper things of the soul. Instead, we hurry from the manger to the mall to get our shopping done and from the gift of Jesus to the wrapping paper of Earth to put presents under the tree. Andrea has thought deeply and written clearly in order to touch our hearts with life-changing insights of the most wonderful time of the year. So slow down, breathe deeply, and enjoy the journey through these pages."

—**Greg Matte,**
Pastor of Houston's First Baptist Church

"It is so easy to get swept up in the tinsel of Christmas and forget to reflect on why this holiday is so rich with meaning. Andrea has written a thoughtful devotional, weaving memorable symbols with tradition and Scripture, all pointing us to the Lord, the source of every good and perfect gift."

—**Joyce Williams,**
Chairwoman of the Board of Directors of the Seed Company,
a Bible Translation Company

"Spending time reading *Our Gift-Giving God* will be one of the most wonderful things you do this Christmas season. Andrea Kim thoughtfully and inspiringly unwraps some of God's most wonderful gifts for His children in a way that will leave you amazed. You'll feel like you just mined treasure from a cave as she takes you to deep and profound places in Scripture. Pour yourself a cup of hot coffee or tea, curl up in a cozy spot, and let the beauty of who God is and what He's done for you fill your heart with wonder."

—**Leigh Kohler,**
Executive Director of Freedom Church Alliance
(Churches United to End Human Trafficking)

OUR
GIFT-GIVING
GOD

A DEVOTIONAL

ANDREA LEVIN KIM
ARTWORK BY CARISSA ROBERTSON

LUCIDBOOKS

Our Gift-Giving God
A Devotional

Copyright © 2018 by Andrea Levin Kim
Artwork by Carissa Robertson

Published by Lucid Books in Houston, TX
www.LucidBooksPublishing.com

ISBN-10: 1-63296-318-3
ISBN-13: 978-1-63296-318-5
eISBN-10: 1-63296-271-3
eISBN-13: 978-1-63296-271-3

Special Sales: Most Lucid Books titles are available in special quantity discounts. Custom imprinting or excerpting can also be done to fit special needs. Contact Lucid Books at Info@ LucidBooksPublishing.com.

Let God Capture Your Heart

&

Transform Your *Christmas Traditions*

Into

Reminders of *Gospel Gifts*

*I dedicate this devotional to the men and women all over the world who choose
to spend their lives translating or helping translate the precious, powerful, life-changing,
eternity-saving words of the Bible, the best seller of all best sellers.[1] They work so more
than 100 million people who have no access to Scripture in their heart languages
will experience, for the first time, the God of the universe speaking to them intimately
in the language they learned to trust from birth. They are making it possible for
the gift of God's promises to be unwrapped in communities many of us may
never visit or even hear of, but that are filled with precious souls in need of hope.*

*There are more than 2,500 active translation projects worldwide and
still more than 2,000 languages in which not a word of Scripture has been translated,
including deaf languages and oral cultures. All net proceeds of this book go to support
The Seed Company, a Bible translation ministry with more than 800 active
translation projects all over the world (http://www.seedcompany.com).*

Thank you for helping give away the most precious gift of hope.

---

1. This dedication is for people just like Kwame Nkrumah, who wrote the foreword to this book. Kwame is a translator who speaks nine languages and has oversight responsibility for 40 translation projects, including translating the Bible into *his* heart language, Delo.

TABLE OF CONTENTS

FOREWORD

If my memory serves me right, I can confidently say I have witnessed, participated in, and celebrated 50 Christmas occasions in my life. These celebrations have all been celebrated in Africa, most of them in Ghana, my homeland.

Christmas has always been a time for good food and plenty of meat—especially meals in the village—a new dress, merrymaking, and exchanging gifts. It is also a time to reunite with family and have fun.

A few of the celebrations have been occasions to reflect on the meaning of Jesus's birth, but this reflection came later in my life.

As I read *Our Gift-Giving God*, a devotional written by Andrea Kim, I could not help but agree with Andrea, especially as she shared the various gifts embedded in Christmas.

God has firmly planted His children. He feeds us daily and makes us fruitful in His vineyard. He has not left us alone to go through life. He has made us into new creatures and given us a new beginning. As we walk with Him in this new life, we have His approval, His stamp of authority that makes us bold to face challenges. This we do joyfully with friendly attitudes. In His great mercy, He provides all that we need to go through life. We have His protection all day long, and above all, He offers us hope—the hope of being with Him eternally.

Giving gifts is a characteristic feature of Christmas. The receiver is always excited even before unwrapping a gift. But the receiver feels even more excitement when the gift meets a need. God's gift of His Son has indeed met a need in our lives, and no other gift can be compared.

In my more than 30 years in Bible translation ministry, I have seen many communities unwrap God's gift of Scripture with great joy and excitement. Receiving the Scripture causes a whole day's celebration. When the Bible translation is completed for a community and the time comes for a community to unwrap this gift, my mind always goes to how we unwrap gifts at Christmas. The family gathers around one another, and each gift is unwrapped amidst joy and laughter. In a similar way, when the community meets to unwrap the gift of God's Word, there is joy, laughter, celebration, and thanksgiving. People can therefore say "Jesus is no longer a stranger" when they realize that the gift is God Himself through His Word. Their hearts are captured by God, and their lives will be transformed as a result of receiving this precious gift.

This devotional brings to life not just the receipt of a gift but the inner satisfaction that accompanies it.

Andrea presents to us the greatest gift of all time, so let us unwrap it daily as we think of Christmas and allow it to transform us into Christ's likeness. Our lives will never be the same.

Blessings,
Sylvester Kwame Nkrumah
Director of Field Programs for the Ghana Institute of Linguistics,
Literacy and Bible Translation

HOW TO USE THIS DEVOTIONAL

In the pages that follow, there are eight gifts to help you prepare your heart for the last gift: the gift of Christmas. Each gift comes with (1) a descriptive narrative about the gift; (2) a summary of the narrative followed by the Bible verses discussed; (3) a few thought-provoking questions about the gift; and (4) a prayer of thanks for the gift. Each gift is also paired with a holiday symbol.

Gift #	Symbol	Gift
1		Firmly Planted, Fed, and Fruitful
2		New Beginnings
3		Approval
4		Joy
5		Friendship
6		Provision
7		Mercy
8		Protection
The Christmas Gift		Hope

How you enjoy the eight gifts and the final gift of Christmas is up to you. But here are a few suggestions:

1. **Savor the Savior:** Savor each gift for three days each from December 1–24.
   a. **Day 1–Receive the Gift:** Read about the gift.
   b. **Day 2–Unwrap the Gift:** Read the brief summary of the gift and the Scriptures it references. You could invite family members to take turns reading verses.
   c. **Day 3–Enjoy the Gift:** On the third day, use the thought questions to savor the gift, and pray the prayers of thanks for it.

The schedule would look like this:

December 1–3: Gift 1

December 4–6: Gift 2

December 7–9: Gift 3

December 10–12: Gift 4

December 13–15: Gift 5

December 16–18: Gift 6

December 19–21: Gift 7

December 22–24: Gift 8

December 25: Gift of Christmas

2. **Eight Days of Gift-Giving:** Hannukah is the Jewish celebration of one of many of God's miracles—the miracle of making the lamp oil last for eight days while the temple was rebuilt. Choose eight days to enjoy the eight gifts, expecting to unwrap a miracle each day—a light to build up your faith.

3. **Celebrate by Symbol:** Enjoy the gift associated with the Christmas tree while putting up a tree. Enjoy the gift associated with scents of Christmas while lighting a scented candle, and so on. Make the symbols come alive with the true gift of Christmas.

INTRODUCTION

In the United States and around the world, Christmas comes with a lot of traditions that can be joy-filled. But like anything else we use to create our own lasting joy and peace, they fall short of the mark. Eventually, the traditions may feel stale, unsatisfying, or even burdensome.

This devotional links treasured traditions—from the Christmas tree, to caroling, and the symbols of them you see throughout the Christmas season— to the deeper, life-giving, hope-producing, beauty-inspiring, healing meaning that the earthly arrival of Jesus Christ is meant to fill us with—not for a season, but for an eternity.

Symbols are meaningful and can be powerful communicators in our lives. Each familiar symbol of the season can begin this Christmas to bring to your mind the powerful, life-changing promise of the gift we've been given in the gospel.

Christmas can be consumed with consumerism and buying, wrapping, giving, and opening presents. It can also be consumed with loss, regret, or struggle. But the only thing that can consume you at Christmas without leaving you empty in the post-tinsel, tree-recycling days that follow the season is the presence of the ultimate Gift-Giver.

Refresh your soul as you practice being in the presence of the King of Kings, Lord of Lords, Emmanuel (God with us) and open just a few of the extravagant gifts that He—and He alone—gives us freely and joyfully. The word *minhâ* in Hebrew, used more than 200 times in the Old Testament, has the basic meaning of *gift*.[1] The word is used to describe offerings, including the grain offering the Jewish people were to voluntarily bring to the tabernacle (temple) to recognize God's goodness and provision, a physical showing of their devotion to Him. The Lord's ultimate offering, His ultimate gift, His ultimate *minhâ*, was His offering of Himself. "He doesn't need to offer sacrifices every day, as high priests do—first for their own sins, then for those of the people. He did this once for all time when he *offered himself*" (Heb. 7:27, emphasis added).

As you "open" these gifts, whether for the first time or the thousandth time, you'll have the opportunity to build up a more grateful heart. It's now been scientifically proven that having a grateful state of mind benefits your relationships as well as your physical, psychological, and mental health, including your sleep.[2] It should be no surprise that we operate best when we operate as the Creator intended.

I pray this devotional will help you unwrap the greatest gift of all time, the gospel gift of Christmas, for you and your friends and family.

GIFT #1: FIRMLY PLANTED, FED, AND FRUITFUL
Luke 2, Isaiah 61:1–3,10, Psalm 1, Psalm 52

Christmas trees, like most traditions, have a colorful past. Before the first Christmas in a manger, people decorated with evergreens at the winter solstice. The solstice, December 21 or 22, the day with the shortest daylight and longest night in the Northern Hemisphere, is very near the date we celebrate Christmas. The evergreen decorations symbolized life and hope, and in some cultures, evergreens themselves were worshipped. Yes, tree worship. In other cultures, greenery represented the return or rejuvenation of their god, a sun god for the Egyptians or an agriculture god for the early Romans. For some, the greenery was believed to scare away demons. Evergreen branches were also symbols of everlasting life.

The Christmas tree tradition we know now started in Germany during the 1500s. It is generally believed that Martin Luther, a Protestant reformer of that day, first added lighted candles to a tree to recreate the inspirational scene of the Creator's handiwork of stars among the evergreen trees that Luther found beautiful. In the United States, however, this tradition did not easily take hold, as American Christians associated the trees with pagan tradition well into the 1800s. In some places, they were illegal, a prohibited heathen tradition. But when Queen Victoria and Prince Albert of Germany adopted the Christmas tree, it caught on as the fashion on the US East Coast and has since been part of the Christmas tradition in not only the United States but also in many countries.[1]

The Lord has use for a tree as
a symbol in our lives.
As you set up your tree or sit by it,
read about its deeper significance.

Some 700 years before the first Christmas, Isaiah wrote down Jesus's mission statement:

> *¹ The Spirit of the Lord GOD is on me, because the LORD has anointed me to bring good news to the poor. He has sent me to heal the brokenhearted, to proclaim liberty to the captives and freedom to the prisoners; ² to proclaim the year of the LORD's favor, and the day of our God's vengeance; to comfort all who mourn, ³ to provide for those who mourn in Zion; to give them a crown of beauty instead of ashes, festive oil instead of mourning, and splendid clothes instead of despair. And they will be called righteous trees, planted by the LORD to glorify him* (Isa. 61:1–3).

Later on and just a few chapters after the Christmas story in Luke 2, Jesus personally read Isaiah 61:1–2 in his local synagogue in Nazareth and proclaimed He had fulfilled the prophecy (Luke 4:17–21). Jesus came with all the wisdom and power of the Father and the Spirit—anointed, chosen, to bring good news to those in distress. At Christmas, God, the very best Gift-Giver, delivered Jesus, whom He calls the Word (John 1:1), the good news, the gospel promise-keeper. Jesus's mission statement in Isaiah 61 shines a light on just how good that news really is. His mission statement had **five points**, just like the star on the top of your tree:

1. He was sent to "heal the brokenhearted"—those who have lost hope, broken by their brokenness, broken by the broken world (Isa. 61:1).

2. He was sent to proclaim freedom to captives and prisoners—those enslaved by their own sin, by the sin of others, bound by a person (captive), place (prisoner), or circumstance (Isa. 61:1, Rom. 6:5–10).

3. He came to announce a long period of blessing (a period in which people could experience salvation) and only a short time of vengeance (a period of tribulation)—a *year* of favor versus a *day* of vengeance (Isa. 61:2).

4. He came to comfort all who mourn. Mourners grieve over a death. He came to comfort those anticipating the death they had earned with their sins (Rom. 3:23). "'*Comfort, comfort* my people,' says your God. 'Speak tenderly to Jerusalem and announce to her that her time of forced labor is over, her iniquity has been pardoned, and she has received from the LORD's hand double for all her sins'" (Isa. 40:1–2, emphasis added).

5. He came to do a major wardrobe change. To replace the ashes, mourning, and despair of the lives of the broken with festive oil, a crown of beauty, and splendid clothes. **Olive oil,** used during festive occasions and as a treatment for an honored guest at a banquet (Luke 7:45–46). A **crown of beauty,** like a bride adorned in jewels (Isa. 61:10). And **splendid clothes** of righteousness replacing our filthy rags of self-righteousness (Isa. 64:6, 61:10, Zech. 3:4).

And then, the finale, the show-stopper, the point when God changes our *identity* from broken mourners, imprisoned in our sin and despair, into something very different. He says that those who were poor in spirit, mourning their sin and situation, who will accept the wardrobe change from self-earned righteousness to Jesus-given righteousness—**they will be called…that's right,** *trees.* "Righteous trees, planted by the LORD to glorify him" (Isa. 61:3). Some translations call them oaks of righteousness.

This is not a grocery store tree popped into a plastic tree stand that squeezes it into upright position by the screws of a vice. This is not a tree planted with stakes in the ground, tied down in hopes it'll grow and not fall over. And this certainly isn't a plastic tree pulled out of a box and assembled only to be stuffed back inside the box in the new year. Planted by the gospel in His grace, we're not fake or temporarily propped up by the holiday and a little hope. We have **permanent, unfailing, sturdy** roots.

We're a tree planted by none other than the One who created trees and knows how best to plant them. When we place our faith in the truly spectacular good news of Christmas, God plants us firmly in the grace, peace, and strength of His presence. The good news of the gospel is that although we were far more steeped in enslaving sin than we'll ever understand, we're far more loved and treasured by our righteous Savior than we could ever have hoped for. So much so that He came to live perfectly—because we can't—and take on the full wrath of God—so we wouldn't have to. The gospel is ushered in by Christmas and completed by Easter, but it lasts forever. God plants us to be purposeful and fruitful. He plants us to show off His grace and creation for His glory.

Not only that, but when we keep our roots tapped into Christ, we become a tree worth talking about. **Psalm 1** says that when we attune our minds and hearts to the Lord rather than following the advice or example of the world, and we choose not to stick with knocking-down words but to delight in His building-up Word, we will be like a tree that is:

1. **Firmly planted** – We won't be blown around easily by the whims of the world and circumstances. "He alone is my rock and my salvation, my stronghold; I will not be shaken" (Ps. 62:6).
2. **Fed** – Like a tree strategically planted by plentiful streams of water, we'll never be without the things we need for life and godliness (2 Pet. 1:3).
3. **Fruitful** – We'll be perfectly fruitful. That is, we bear the fruit we're *meant* to bear in the *time* we're meant to bear it, and we will *continue to grow.* Not to drop brown needles or get sent to the chipper, but to mature and be a source of life and comfort to others.

In Psalm 52, the psalmist shows us that if we'll put our full trust *not* in wealth, lies, or manipulation but in the unfailing love of God, we can be like an olive tree flourishing in the house of God. Like an olive tree, we can produce the oil of gladness for eternal Kingdom celebrations today, on Christmas, and for every day to come.

FIRMLY PLANTED, FED, AND FRUITFUL:
GIFT #1 SUMMARY AND SCRIPTURE

SUMMARY

The gospel allows us to overcome the shifting sands of pride or despair as we try to hold others to our flawed standards or meet others' standards. In the gospel, we're rooted in the stable sod of His grace—plentiful, life-giving, fruit-making soil. Apart from God, we're cursed, dirty ground, but with Him, we're free to be fruitful, free from comparison and flawed judgment (ours and others), free to be like a tree—not like the one cut down and popped in water for December and thrown away, but like one *rooted for eternity*.

SCRIPTURES FOR GIFT #1

Isaiah 61:1–3

¹ The Spirit of the Lord God is on me, because the Lord has anointed me to bring good news to the poor. He has sent me to heal the brokenhearted, to proclaim liberty to the captives and freedom to the prisoners; ² to proclaim the year of the Lord's favor, and the day of our God's vengeance; to comfort all who mourn, ³ to provide for those who mourn in Zion; to give them a crown of beauty instead of ashes, festive oil instead of mourning, and splendid clothes instead of despair. And they will be called righteous trees, planted by the Lord to glorify him.

Luke 4:17–21

¹⁷ The scroll of the prophet Isaiah was given to him, and unrolling the scroll, he found the place where it was written:

¹⁸ **The Spirit of the Lord is on me,**
because he has anointed me
to preach good news to the poor.
He has sent me
to proclaim release to the captives
and recovery of sight to the blind,
to set free the oppressed,
¹⁹ **to proclaim the year of the Lord's favor.**

²⁰ He then rolled up the scroll, gave it back to the attendant, and sat down. And the eyes of everyone in the synagogue were fixed on him. ²¹ He began by saying to them, "Today as you listen, this Scripture has been fulfilled."

Romans 6:5–10

[5] For if we have been united with him in the likeness of his death, we will certainly also be in the likeness of his resurrection. [6] For we know that our old self was crucified with him so that the body ruled by sin might be rendered powerless so that we may no longer be enslaved to sin, [7] since a person who has died is freed from sin. [8] Now if we died with Christ, we believe that we will also live with him, [9] because we know that Christ, having been raised from the dead, will not die again. Death no longer rules over him. [10] For the death he died, he died to sin once for all time; but the life he lives, he lives to God.

Romans 3:23

[23] For all have sinned and fall short of the glory of God.

Isaiah 40:1–2

[1] "Comfort, comfort my people," says your God. [2] "Speak tenderly to Jerusalem, and announce to her that her time of forced labor is over, her iniquity has been pardoned, and she has received from the Lord's hand double for all her sins."

Isaiah 64:6

[6] All of us have become like something unclean,
and all our righteous acts are like a polluted garment;
all of us wither like a leaf,
and our iniquities carry us away like the wind.

Zechariah 3:4

[4] So the angel of the Lord spoke to those standing before him, "Take off his filthy clothes!" Then he said to him, "See, I have removed your iniquity from you, and I will clothe you with festive robes."

Isaiah 61:10

[10] I rejoice greatly in the Lord,
I exult in my God;
for he has clothed me with the garments of salvation
and wrapped me in a robe of righteousness,
as a groom wears a turban
and as a bride adorns herself with her jewels.

Psalm 1

[1] How happy is the one who does not walk in the advice of the wicked or stand in the pathway with sinners or sit in the company of mockers!

² Instead, his delight is in the LORD's instruction, and he meditates on it day and night.

³ He is like a tree planted beside flowing streams that bears its fruit in its season and whose leaf does not wither. Whatever he does prospers.

⁴ The wicked are not like this; instead, they are like chaff that the wind blows away.

⁵ Therefore the wicked will not stand up in the judgment, nor sinners in the assembly of the righteous.

⁶ For the LORD watches over the way of the righteous, but the way of the wicked leads to ruin.

Psalm 62:6

² He alone is my rock and my salvation, my stronghold; I will not be shaken.

2 Peter 1:3

³ His divine power has given us everything required for life and godliness through the knowledge of him who called us by his own glory and goodness.

Psalm 52:8–9

⁸ But I am like a flourishing olive tree in the house of God; I trust in God's faithful love forever and ever.

⁹ I will praise you forever for what you have done. In the presence of your faithful people, I will put my hope in your name, for it is good.

John 1:1

¹ In the beginning was the Word, and the Word was with God, and the Word was God.

Luke 2:1- 20

¹ In those days a decree went out from Caesar Augustus that the whole empire should be registered. ² This first registration took place while Quirinius was governing Syria. ³ So everyone went to be registered, each to his own town.

⁴ Joseph also went up from the town of Nazareth in Galilee, to Judea, to the city of David, which is called Bethlehem, because he was of the house and family line of David, ⁵ to be registered along with Mary, who was engaged to him and was pregnant. ⁶ While they were there, the time came for her to give birth. ⁷ Then she gave birth to her firstborn Son, and she wrapped him tightly in cloth and laid him in a manger, because there was no guest room available for them.

⁸ In the same region, shepherds were staying out in the fields and keeping watch at night over their flock. ⁹ Then an angel of the Lord stood before them, and the

glory of the Lord shone around them, and they were terrified. [10] But the angel said to them, "Don't be afraid, for look, I proclaim to you good news of great joy that will be for all the people: [11] Today in the city of David a Savior was born for you, who is the Messiah, the Lord. [12] This will be the sign for you: You will find a baby wrapped tightly in cloth and lying in a manger."

[13] Suddenly there was a multitude of the heavenly host with the angel, praising God and saying:

[14] Glory to God in the highest heaven,

and peace on earth to people he favors!

[15] When the angels had left them and returned to heaven, the shepherds said to one another, "Let's go straight to Bethlehem and see what has happened, which the Lord has made known to us."

[16] They hurried off and found both Mary and Joseph, and the baby who was lying in the manger. [17] After seeing them, they reported the message they were told about this child, [18] and all who heard it were amazed at what the shepherds said to them. [19] But Mary was treasuring up all these things in her heart and meditating on them. [20] The shepherds returned, glorifying and praising God for all the things they had seen and heard, which were just as they had been told.

FIRMLY PLANTED, FED, AND FRUITFUL:
GIFT #1 REFLECTION AND PRAYER

REFLECTION QUESTIONS

1. **Firmly Planted:** Recall a time when you felt the people around you or your circumstances were blowing you in one direction and then another, changing your mind, your peace, and your stability. How might that experience have been different if you had trusted that you're like a tree deeply rooted in God's grace for eternity, and your future can't be uprooted?

2. **Fed:** Ever been super thirsty with no drink in sight? Thirst can consume you until it is quenched. It can interfere with thinking clearly and sap your energy. Our access to Christ is like a tree's roots having permanent access to streams of water. When we spend time with Him in prayer, read His Word, and trust Him day by day, we reach out to the water source. Ponder how your life and relationship with the Lord might look like thirst (a distracted, exhausted state dying for the Lord's graceful presence) or like abundant streams (overflowing to others what He's pouring into you).

   But whoever drinks from the water that I will give him will never get thirsty again. In fact, the water I will give him will become a well of water springing up in him for eternal life (John 4:14).

3. **Fruitful:** For an actual tree to bear fruit, during its first few years the blossoms or fruit have to be snipped off so the nutrients go *down* to grow the roots instead of *up* to fill the fruit. Is the Lord pruning you to grow your roots so they reach deeper into Christ? How do you see your life bearing the fruit of love for others, especially the hard-to-love, tough nuts?

PRAYER

Father, I place all my trust and hope in the great news of the gospel message that Christ was not just born a gift but died taking the full force of Your righteous judgment for all sin and was resurrected a fully-accepted sacrifice. Help me to **celebrate** the radical wardrobe change Jesus provided and to be deeply **rooted** in Your Word, Your love letter, so I can enjoy the beautiful gift You have given me of being **firmly planted, fed, and fruitful**.

GIFT #2: NEW BEGINNINGS
Leviticus 1, 6:8–13, 2 Corinthians 5:21, Hebrews 10:1–18

In some climates and many homes, a fireplace is only minimally useful and maybe isn't present at all. But many Christmas scenes around the world involve the hearth as the symbolic warm heart of the home, decorated with lights, garlands, and stockings. Some homes might even have a gas log fireplace so the owners can dodge the unpleasant task of cleaning the fireplace ashes.

But the Christmas coming of the Lord Jesus Christ
has a lot to do with what happens when real burning
produces real ashes. As you sit around or decorate
your fireplace or a symbolic place of gathering,
read about God's gift of a burnt offering.

For hundreds of years after Moses led the exodus out of Egypt, the Lord led the Jewish people in sacrificial offerings in anticipation of the first Christmas. These offerings were a critical part of everyday life, and God's chosen priests facilitated the sacrifices. There were (1) sacrifices of animals, spilled blood required in payment for sin (sin and guilt offerings); (2) sacrifices for His people to show their dedication (burnt and grain offerings); and (3) sacrifices to restore fellowship or communion with the Lord (fellowship offerings).

The **burnt offering** was listed first among the offerings the Lord prescribed. It was the most common. Unlike the sin and guilt offerings, which were *mandatory* atonements to temporarily deal with the offeror's sin, the burnt offering was *voluntary*. It was the offering, the sacrifice, used to voluntarily consecrate or dedicate oneself completely to God. In effect, the worshipper brought burnt offerings as a statement of devotion and surrender.

15

The worshipper, of his or her own will, chose to bring a perfect animal to the tent of meeting—the Israelites' meeting place with the Lord. Leviticus 1:4 describes how he or she would then lay hands on the animal's head, but the Hebrew word here for *lay* really means applying pressure or leaning on something. Worshippers put their weight, their full self, their full trust in the acceptance of the sacrifice being made, and the sacrifice was accepted on the worshipper's behalf.[1] The worshipper would then take the young animal's life. This was a painful, ugly sacrifice of a perfect life. The priest would then sprinkle the animal's blood on the altar on all sides, and it would be laid on the wood fire to burn throughout the night. The worshipper would return home, trusting fully in God's acceptance of that sacrifice to pay for the gap between his or her flawed, imperfect dedication to God and the full, perfect measure of surrender to God that He deserves.

In the morning, the worshippers gone, the priest was left with the ashes. He didn't make the ashes, but he was responsible for removing them. Obeying the Lord's specific instruction, the priest would do something we would not. He put on **white linen clothes to shovel the ashes**. A strange wardrobe choice for dirty work! If you've ever shoveled ashes, you know that they easily fly up and attach themselves everywhere, soiling everything in their wake. In a house fire, soot is carried through the air to cover every nook and cranny of the house, even the places where the fire was not burning (see Exod. 9:8–10).

But the removal of the ashes was holy work. In fact, once the priest had put the ashes beside the altar, he'd change out of his linen to carry the ashes outside the camp to a ceremonially cleansed place and then put new firewood on the fire. In the whole process of administering the burnt offering, the priest put on the white linen garb only to remove the ashes. A simple task. An impractical outfit. But God's clothing choice for that small but very significant task is laden with purpose.

By commanding the priests to wear white linen clothes, which represented purity, holiness, and perfection, God gave us a picture of the one perfect Priest. The perfect Priest whose birth is celebrated every Christmas. The One who would be perfect and holy and would shine with glory. The One whose body would be wrapped in strips of that linen in death, but those strips of linen could not hold His glory (John 19:40, 20:6). The only One who can shovel out and completely remove the ashes of our grief and replace them with a crown of beauty (Isa. 61:3). The only One we can lean on with the full weight of our trust and faith, counting on Him to be our payment for sin. The only One who willingly would let the filth of *our* ashes cover *His* holiness so *we* could wear white linen before the Lord (2 Cor. 5:21). The only One who is able to take the ashes—the sticky, messy, smelly, invasive, smothering, fast-spreading remnants of our sin—and rescue us from their stench, removing any evidence of them from our soul.

The sacrificial offerings were a shadow, hinting at the ultimate sacrifice for sin that God introduced to humankind, in person, at the first Christmas. It would be the painful sacrifice of a perfect life, the sacrifice that would be one sacrifice for all sins: the sacrifice of Jesus Christ on the cross. Jesus came at Christmas, destined to ultimately replace *all* of the Old Testament sacrifices. Hebrews 10:1–18 explains that Jesus alone atoned for our sins once and for all. "For by one sacrifice He has made perfect forever those who are being made holy. And where these have been forgiven, sacrifice for sin is no longer necessary" (Heb. 10:14,18 NIV).

When we sin again and again, falling short of the devotion and surrender to God that He deserves, we create more ashes. But when we bring our ashes to Him, He is faithful to carry them out again and again. "If we confess our sins, he is faithful and righteous to forgive us our sins and to cleanse us from all unrighteousness" (1 John 1:9).

During the Christmas season, you'll see countless scenes of white, snowy nights and warm fires, whether in real life or on screens. If you light a clean fireplace this Christmas, whether cleansed of past ashes or an ash-free gas log, let the occasion remind you of the **new beginning**, and continued new beginnings, that God gives you. The precious gift of a new beginning made possible by Christmas and Easter. Jesus is the chimney sweep of your soul, and the author and perfecter of the faith you have in Him that makes you clean (Heb. 12:1–2).

Maybe, like the fireplace, you think your soul is the *last* place you'd expect to be squeaky clean. Maybe you can't even imagine what that fireplace looked like before it was covered in soot, before it was covered in shame or the stain of past and present mistakes. Maybe you've given up trying to fight the soot or think it's too late to try. Maybe the soot feels somehow more comfortable and familiar. But this Christmas, let God give you the **gift of a new beginning** with Him, who looks through His Son Jesus and sees a squeaky. clean. you.

NEW BEGINNINGS:
GIFT #2 SUMMARY AND SCRIPTURE

SUMMARY

We need not wait for New Year's resolutions to celebrate a new beginning, a do-over. A new beginning is the very thing that makes a new year so special, but it is actually a Christmas gift from the greatest Gift-Giver of all time. The Old Testament's sacrificial offerings provide a vivid picture of the ugliness and grief involved in rectifying our sin in order to restore our precious relationship with that very holy, perfect, gift-giving God. The offerings foreshadowed the cost of our new beginnings on the cross. But like a worshipper bringing a burnt offering, we voluntarily come into the presence of God by laying the full weight of our faith on Jesus as our perfect sacrifice. We count on God's acceptance of that sacrifice, His refining fire, and our perfect Priest, Jesus Christ, to clean out the ash and soot of sin from our soul so we can be presented to God forever dressed in clothes of righteousness. He is faithful to forgive us and give us the power and beauty of His holy presence as we confess our sin to Him because He loves us in God-sized proportions.

SCRIPTURES FOR GIFT #2

Leviticus 1:1–9

¹ Then the LORD summoned Moses and spoke to him from the tent of meeting: ² "Speak to the Israelites and tell them: When any of you brings an offering to the LORD from the livestock, you may bring your offering from the herd or the flock.

³ If his offering is a burnt offering from the herd, he is to bring an unblemished male. He will bring it to the entrance to the tent of meeting so that he may be accepted by the LORD. ⁴ He is to lay his hand on the head of the burnt offering so it can be accepted on his behalf to make atonement for him. ⁵ He is to slaughter the bull before the LORD; Aaron's sons the priests are to present the blood and splatter it on all sides of the altar that is at the entrance to the tent of meeting. ⁶ Then he is to skin the burnt offering and cut it into pieces. ⁷ The sons of Aaron the priest will prepare a fire on the altar and arrange wood on the fire. ⁸ Aaron's sons the priests are to arrange the pieces, the head, and the fat on top of the burning wood on the altar. ⁹ The offerer is to wash its entrails and legs with water. Then the priest will burn all of it on the altar as a burnt offering, a fire offering of a pleasing aroma to the LORD."

Leviticus 6:8–13

⁸ The LORD spoke to Moses: ⁹ "Command Aaron and his sons: This is the law of the burnt offering; the burnt offering itself must remain on the altar's hearth all night

until morning, while the fire of the altar is kept burning on it. ¹⁰ The priest is to put on his linen robe and linen undergarments. He is to remove the ashes of the burnt offering the fire has consumed on the altar, and place them beside the altar. ¹¹ Then he will take off his garments, put on other clothes, and bring the ashes outside the camp to a ceremonially clean place. ¹² The fire on the altar is to be kept burning; it must not go out. Every morning the priest will burn wood on the fire. He is to arrange the burnt offering on the fire and burn the fat portions from the fellowship offerings on it. ¹³ Fire must be kept burning on the altar continually; it must not go out."

Exodus 9:8–10

⁸ Then the LORD said to Moses and Aaron, "Take handfuls of furnace soot, and Moses is to throw it toward heaven in the sight of Pharaoh. ⁹ It will become fine dust over the entire land of Egypt. It will become festering boils on people and animals throughout the land of Egypt." ¹⁰ So they took furnace soot and stood before Pharaoh. Moses threw it toward heaven, and it became festering boils on people and animals.

John 19:40

⁴⁰ They took Jesus's body and wrapped it in linen cloths with the fragrant spices, according to the burial custom of the Jews.

John 20:6

⁶ Then, following him, Simon Peter also came. He entered the tomb and saw the linen cloths lying there.

Isaiah 61:1–3

¹ The Spirit of the Lord GOD is on me, because the LORD has anointed me to bring good news to the poor. He has sent me to heal the brokenhearted, to proclaim liberty to the captives and freedom to the prisoners; ² to proclaim the year of the LORD's favor, and the day of our God's vengeance; to comfort all who mourn, ³ to provide for those who mourn in Zion; to give them a crown of beauty instead of ashes, festive oil instead of mourning, and splendid clothes instead of despair. And they will be called righteous trees, planted by the LORD to glorify him.

Hebrews 10:1–18

¹ Since the law has only a shadow of the good things to come, and not the reality itself of those things, it can never perfect the worshipers by the same sacrifices they continually offer year after year. ² Otherwise, wouldn't they have stopped being offered, since the worshipers, purified once and for all, would no longer have any consciousness

of sins? [3] But in the sacrifices there is a reminder of sins year after year. [4] For it is impossible for the blood of bulls and goats to take away sins.

[5] Therefore, as he was coming into the world, he said:

> **You did not desire sacrifice and offering, but you prepared a body for me.**
> [6] **You did not delight in whole burnt offerings and sin offerings.**
> [7] **Then I said, "See—it is written about me in the scroll—I have come to do your will, O God."**

[8] After he says above, **You did not desire or delight in sacrifices and offerings, whole burnt offerings and sin offerings** (which are offered according to the law), [9] he then says, **See, I have come to do your will.** He takes away the first to establish the second. [10] By this will, we have been sanctified through the offering of the body of Jesus Christ once for all time.

[11] Every priest stands day after day ministering and offering the same sacrifices time after time, which can never take away sins. [12] But this man, after offering one sacrifice for sins forever, sat down at the right hand of God. [13] He is now waiting until his enemies are made his footstool. [14] For by one offering he has perfected forever those who are sanctified. [15] The Holy Spirit also testifies to us about this. For after he says:

> [16] **This is the covenant I will make with them after those days,**
> **the Lord says,**
> **I will put my laws on their hearts and write them on their minds,**
> [17] **and I will never again remember**
> **their sins** and their lawless acts.

[18] Now where there is forgiveness of these, there is no longer an offering for sin.

1 John 1:9

[9] If we confess our sins, he is faithful and just and will forgive us our sins and purify us from all unrighteousness.

Hebrews 12:1–2 NIV

[1] Therefore, since we are surrounded by such a great cloud of witnesses, let us throw off everything that hinders and the sin that so easily entangles. And let us run with perseverance the race marked out for us, [2] fixing our eyes on Jesus, the pioneer and perfecter of faith. For the joy set before him he endured the cross, scorning its shame, and sat down at the right hand of the throne of God.

2 Corinthians 5:21

[21] He made the one who did not know sin to be sin for us, so that in him we might become the righteousness of God.

NEW BEGINNINGS:
GIFT #2 REFLECTION AND PRAYER

REFLECTION QUESTIONS

1. What holds you back from grasping hold of a new beginning with God? Do you worry about strings attached to the gift of a new beginning? Worried what he might ask in return? Do you struggle to believe He would give you such an unmerited gift? Take a moment to write down the beliefs and concerns keeping you from accepting His free gift of a new beginning that comes with the simple faith in Christ as your Rescuer and Savior. Ask God to remove your concerns. If you have a fireplace handy, toss your list of new-beginning speed bumps into the fire.

2. Are there moments in the past you'd like to redo? We can't change the past, but Jesus is able to completely forgive and redeem all our past mistakes. How does that fact alone bring new hope and new passion?

3. Sin—our sin and the sin in the world—is complicated, messy, and sticky, and it produces breath-choking, soul-staining, life-smothering results. We don't want to even think about it, let alone confess it. But as we confess where we've gone astray from the God that loves us so deeply, the soot lifts, and we can take a deep, clean breath and restore our soul. Take a few moments to privately consider what sins you can confess so you can experience the Lord lifting the ash from you. What would your life look like free from those ashes? What habits, relationships, and fears might be swept away?

4. Lean in and lean on. Trust is hard. Putting all your eggs in any basket and committing to one path or one person can be scary. Find a very stable chair or sofa, or even use the floor, and put all your weight on it. Think about your trust in that object to hold you up as a symbol for relying on God. Ask the Lord to help you trust Him in the same way, putting your full faith in Him and in the sacrifice of your Savior to make you clean in God's eyes.

5. Do you find yourself still living in the shame dust of past mistakes, failures, and sins? Are your regrets or mistakes dictating your thoughts and actions, or are you fueled by gratitude for full forgiveness?

PRAYER

Lord, thank you that regardless of whether my fireplace is clean (if I even have one), my soul can be, despite myself. Thank You for the gift of a new beginning today; thank You that You give me the ability to stand in Your holy presence and renew my commitment and devotion to You, and graciously accept me on account of the sacrifice of Your Son. Help me come to know my perfect Priest ever more deeply and intimately as He removes the ashes of my sin as far as the east is from the west.

GIFT #3: APPROVAL
Genesis 8:6–12, 1 Peter 3:18–22, Matthew 3:16–17, Galatians 1:10

What if someone could give you the gift of approval for Christmas? What would you think of the gift-wrapped guarantee that your parents, siblings, spouse, friends, coworkers, teachers, and boss would *approve* of you? Fully approve of you. Declare once and for all that you are enough and meet *all* their expectations.

That would be a tall order because parents, siblings, spouses, friends, coworkers, teachers, and bosses are *people*. People are imperfect. They change their minds and moods, fail to communicate their expectations, and even shift their expectations, some of which may be a little unrealistic. Then, of course, choosing *whose* expectations to meet would be even tougher, since the expectations of all those people would conflict. And then there's the problem that some folks' expectations of you would require you to do and say things that are not true. That you don't believe. That are just wrong. So let's just scratch that wish off the Christmas list (Gal. 1:10).

But what if you could open a package filled with the **guaranteed approval** of God? The total approval of the perfectly holy, perfectly just, perfectly loving, unchanging, all-powerful, all-knowing, all-seeing, Creator of the universe? Try to imagine it. What if this Christmas you opened His stamp of approval? What would the inside of that package look like? Can you imagine it? What if you opened up that box, and like a magician's assistant reaching into a hat, inside you found…**a DOVE**?

On Christmas cards and even agnostic "holiday" cards, on tree ornaments and in Christmas carols, the dove shakes a tail feather and makes quite an appearance. In the familiar song "The Twelve Days of Christmas," the singer's true love gives the gift of a partridge in a pear tree on the first day. (Tough to pull off, really. How did they get the bird to stay in the tree?) But on the second day, the true love ups the ante and gives the gift of two turtledoves. The *turtle* part of the name comes from the sound they make (not the slow, green, hard-shelled critter). The turtledove is a familiar sight. It's the dove that's on everything from candy to peace treaties.

The dove is more of a Christmas bird
than you might think. Read about
how you can find it printed on the wrappings
of God's full approval.

As Jesus came out of the water of His baptism in the Jordan River, the heavens opened and the Holy Spirit descended on Him, appearing in the shape of a dove. At that moment, God the Father audibly spoke, "This is my beloved Son, with whom I am well-pleased" (Matt. 3:17). Now *that* is **one. spectacular. stamp of approval.** But why did the Holy Spirit appear in that form? The Holy Spirit did not need to appear at all. He could have descended on Jesus without anyone seeing Him or come in the form of something else, maybe a fluffy cloud or a fierce fire. Why a dove?

Thousands of years before Jesus's baptism on Earth, the Lord had to deal with a wholly fallen, violent, wicked creation. God found one man, a man of faith, and his family to rescue. They were a remnant of faith with which to start again. So He instructed that man to build a rescue vessel of gargantuan proportions and fill it with two of every kind of creature, as well as his family. Then, after 120 years of patiently waiting for others to come to faith and join the rescued, God Himself locked the ark up tight to keep that remnant safe and sound during the storm of His righteous wrath.

When Noah and his family made it through the storm, a storm that demanded the life of every living being outside the ark to atone for the wickedness on Earth (Gen. 6:11–13, 7:22–23), Noah sent out winged scouts to look for dry ground (Gen. 8:6–12). First, he sent a raven that flew around until the water receded. Then he sent a dove, but the dove couldn't find a place to land. There was not yet exposed dry land, as the whole globe was covered with water. So he took the dove in again. A week later, he tried again with the dove, and the dove dutifully returned with an olive leaf or branch in its bill (Gen. 8:10–11).

When Noah saw that the dove had found dry land, he knew God's righteous wrath had been satisfied: the water had receded. **The earth's cleansing baptism was over** (Gen 8:6–12, 1 Pet. 3:18–22).

To understand the dove's command performance for Christ's baptism as well as for giving Noah the all clear, we need to listen to Peter link the two events. Peter, perhaps Jesus's most impetuous follower-turned-powerful apostle, understood well that the dove's appearance at both events was no accident. He explained:

¹⁸ For Christ also suffered once for sins, the righteous for the unrighteous, to bring you to God. He was put to death in the body but made alive in the Spirit. ¹⁹ After being made alive, he went and made proclamation to the imprisoned spirits— ²⁰ to those who were disobedient long ago when God waited patiently in the days of Noah while the ark was being built. In it only a few people, eight in all, were saved through water, ²¹ and this water symbolizes baptism that now saves you also—not the removal of dirt from the body but the pledge of a clear conscience toward God. It saves you by the resurrection of Jesus Christ, ²² who has gone into heaven and is at God's right hand— with angels, authorities and powers in submission to him (1 Pet. 3:18–22 NIV).

Peter knew that Noah's life of faith and God's approval of Jesus at His baptism had several important things in common—not just the bird.

1. **Saved by Grace through Faith in the Lord as Savior**

First, when Noah put his faith in the Lord, he and his seven family members were saved. Noah had to practice faith to believe God. Faith to build a boat. Faith to get in. Faith in the Lord as Savior. The dove came as an announcement of the culmination of his faith in God: his salvation.

Likewise, the dove announced that Jesus was the approved-of sacrifice in whom God was well pleased. When we put our faith in the Lord, by His grace, through this faith, we are saved (Eph. 2:8–9). We practice faith to believe God that Jesus's sacrifice paid the price for our sin (Eph. 2:18). Faith that Jesus was fully accepted by God as sacrifice when He was resurrected (Eph. 2:21). Faith that Jesus's sacrifice alone saves us from the ultimate righteous punishment for sin. The dove came as an announcement of the Savior we could put our faith in.

2. **A Rescue Story**

In Noah's lifetime, God patiently waited 120 years for humankind to believe in Him and turn from their sin, but when none but Noah's family believed, God **rescued** the faithful by boat from His righteous wrath toward sin. When Jesus was baptized at the beginning of his earthly in-person ministry, He was, in effect, rehearsing his death and burial (under the water) and resurrection (coming out of the water). He was **rehearsing God's rescue plan** for us: the death, burial, and resurrection of the Messiah.

3. **Outward Sign of Inward Faith**

Noah and his family's ride on top of the flood waters (and not underneath them) was the *outward sign* of their saving faith in the Lord. It was by God's grace, His unmerited favor toward Noah and his family, and through their faith in the Lord as Savior that they were saved. When we are baptized (underneath, not on top of the water), following Christ's example of baptism, we are *identifying* with His death and resurrection. We are giving an outward sign that we've put our faith in His burial and resurrection as the payment for our sins. We are giving an outward sign that we are willing to die to our own plans and desires and be reborn. We are giving an outward sign that we are His children, pulled from death into eternal life, saved by faith in His sweet grace.

4. The Dove's Arrival

In both cases, the dove's arrival was a sign of peace between God and man. The dove brought the message to Noah that wrath was over. Salvation was here. Peace on Earth. Peace between God and humans had been achieved by the just payment for sin exacted. When the dove arrived and landed on Jesus as He came out of the water of His baptism, it was a sign that with Jesus, with His ultimate sacrifice, God's wrath was over. Salvation was here. Peace on Earth. Peace between God and man had been achieved by the just payment for sin exacted, and—most importantly—God's approval of His perfect Son.

Noah got a fresh start with God's approval, and Jesus began His ministry with God's approval.

How appropriate that Peter would understand so deeply the hope and importance of **God's approval**. Peter, the disciple who so passionately sought Christ's approval but so dismally failed to earn it on his own. Peter, who told Jesus He must *not* go to the cross (Matt. 16:21–23), promised he would never betray Jesus (Matt. 26:35), and defended Jesus with all his might (John 18:10–11, Luke 22:49–51). The same Peter who then turned around and betrayed Jesus three times (John 18:15–27) yet nonetheless was restored, forgiven, and commissioned by Jesus to be an apostle of the gospel.

Peace on Earth is not a status report on the political or social temperature of the planet. It is a declaration that with the Savior's coming, humankind would, by faith and trust in Him and His payment for our sin on the cross, no longer be at odds with God. We would no longer be His enemy at war (Rom. 5:10), but a friend at peace under the covering of His *approved* sacrificed Son. The approval we so desperately wish we could earn, and so deeply need Him to give.

Perhaps we can hope this Christmas to share in Noah's and Peter's deep understanding of our purchased gift of approval, our **purchased peace**. To **count the cost**, as certainly Noah could. Or to appreciate how **we could never earn that approval** on our own, as Peter intimately understood.

God's approval of us was an expensive gift. It cost Him dearly. It cost the Father and the Son separation, albeit a temporary one. Jesus anguished over the pain of the coming separation in the Garden of Gethsemane. He did not fear for His life—He'd put His life in danger every day of His ministry. But He struggled with the pain of taking on the full wrath of God, **separated and disapproved**. He took the disapproval for all our shortcomings and all the violence we would do in our relationships with Him and one another. He took the force, humiliation, and pain of God's **righteous disapproval** so we could enjoy the **peace of His full** *approval.* And he wrapped up this gift for us and gave it to us at no cost to us.

Accepting this gift from the Lord means letting go of endless efforts to win His (and everyone else's) approval. Accepting this gospel gift of approval humbles us and fills us with a deeper desire to love and serve the Giver with all our heart, soul, and mind, and to love others out of that secure place of the covering of His approval. He will never love you less and He cannot love you more because His love and approval are perfect—the tip top, very best stamp of approval there is, the gold star that covers all other gold stars. How rich, how amazing, how unbelievably great is His great gift of approval.

APPROVAL:
GIFT #3 SUMMARY AND SCRIPTURE

SUMMARY

As you hear the words "Peace on Earth, good will to men" and see doves adorn cards and carols this season—as they have for centuries graced everything from peace treaties to Picasso's work (*La Colombe*)—let the peace you enjoy with God, His full, eternal, perfect approval, wash over you like the warmth of the full Son. Let the extravagant nature of the gift, the graciousness of the Giver, the costly nature of it, and the desperate need for it lift its worth in your heart and mind.

SCRIPTURES FOR GIFT #3

Genesis 8:6–21

[6] After forty days Noah opened the window of the ark that he had made, [7] and he sent out a raven. It went back and forth until the water had dried up from the earth. [8] Then he sent out a dove to see whether the water on the earth's surface had gone down, [9] but the dove found no resting place for its foot. It returned to him in the ark because water covered the surface of the whole earth. He reached out and brought it into the ark to himself. [10] So Noah waited seven more days and sent out the dove from the ark again. [11] When the dove came to him at evening, there was a plucked olive leaf in its beak. So Noah knew that the water on the earth's surface had gone down. [12] After he had waited another seven days, he sent out the dove, but it did not return to him again. [13] In the six hundred and first year, in the first month, on the first day of the month, the water that had covered the earth was dried up. Then Noah removed the ark's cover and saw that the surface of the ground was drying. [14] By the twenty-seventh day of the second month, the earth was dry.

[15] Then God spoke to Noah, [16] "Come out of the ark, you, your wife, your sons, and your sons' wives with you. [17] Bring out all the living creatures that are with you—birds, livestock, those that crawl on the earth—and they will spread over the earth and be fruitful and multiply on the earth." [18] So Noah, along with his sons, his wife, and his sons' wives, came out. [19] All the animals, all the creatures that crawl, and all the flying creatures—everything that moves on the earth—came out of the ark by their families.

[20] Then Noah built an altar to the LORD. He took some of every kind of clean animal and every kind of clean bird and offered burnt offerings on the altar. [21] When the LORD smelled the pleasing aroma, he said to himself, "I will never again curse the ground because of human beings, even though the inclination of the human heart is evil from youth onward. And I will never again strike down every living thing as I have done.

Matthew 3:16–17 NIV

[16] As soon as Jesus was baptized, he went up out of the water. At that moment heaven was opened, and he saw the Spirit of God descending like a dove and alighting on him. [17] And a voice from heaven said, "This is my Son, whom I love; with him I am well pleased."

Genesis 6:11–13

[11] Now the earth was corrupt in God's sight, and the earth was filled with wickedness. [12] God saw how corrupt the earth was, for every creature had corrupted its way on the earth. [13] Then God said to Noah, "I have decided to put an end to every creature, for the earth is filled with wickedness because of them; therefore I am going to destroy them along with the earth.

Genesis 7:22–23

[22] Everything with the breath of the spirit of life in its nostrils—everything on dry land died. [23] He wiped out every living thing that was on the face of the earth, from mankind to livestock, to creatures that crawl, to the birds of the sky, and they were wiped off the earth. Only Noah was left, and those that were with him in the ark.

Galatians 1:10 NIV

[10] Am I now trying to win the approval of human beings, or of God? Or am I trying to please people? If I were still trying to please people, I would not be a servant of Christ.

1 Peter 3:18–22

[18] For Christ also suffered for sins once for all, the righteous for the unrighteous, that he might bring you to God. He was put to death in the flesh but made alive by the Spirit, [19] in which he also went and made proclamation to the spirits in prison [20] who in the past were disobedient, when God patiently waited in the days of Noah while the ark was being prepared. In it a few—that is, eight people—were saved through water. [21] Baptism, which corresponds to this, now saves you (not as the removal of dirt from the body, but the pledge of a good conscience toward God) through the resurrection of Jesus Christ, [22] who has gone into heaven and is at the right hand of God with angels, authorities, and powers subject to him.

Ephesians 2:8–9

[8] For you are saved by grace through faith, and this is not from yourselves; it is God's gift— [9] not from works, so that no one can boast.

Matthew 16:21–23

²¹ From then on Jesus began to point out to his disciples that it was necessary for him to go to Jerusalem and suffer many things from the elders, chief priests, and scribes, be killed, and be raised the third day. ²² Peter took him aside and began to rebuke him, "Oh no, Lord! This will never happen to you!"

²³ Jesus turned and told Peter, "Get behind me, Satan! You are a hindrance to me because you're not thinking about God's concerns but human concerns."

Matthew 26:35

³⁵ "Even if I have to die with you," Peter told him, "I will never deny you," and all the disciples said the same thing.

John 18:10–11

¹⁰ Then Simon Peter, who had a sword, drew it, struck the high priest's servant, and cut off his right ear. (The servant's name was Malchus.) ¹¹ At that, Jesus said to Peter, "Put your sword away! Am I not to drink the cup the Father has given me?"

Luke 22:49–51

⁴⁹ When those around him saw what was going to happen, they asked, "Lord, should we strike with the sword?" ⁵⁰ Then one of them struck the high priest's servant and cut off his right ear.

⁵¹ But Jesus responded, "No more of this!" And touching his ear, he healed him.

Romans 5:10 NIV

¹⁰ For if, while we were God's enemies, we were reconciled to him through the death of his Son, how much more, having been reconciled, shall we be saved through his life!

APPROVAL:
GIFT #3 REFLECTION AND PRAYER
REFLECTION QUESTIONS

1. This Christmas season, whose approval do you really want most? Go ahead, be honest. Your parents? Your spouse? Your boss? Your significant other? Take a moment to imagine the scene of that person totally approving of you—the whole package. Feel relieved? Free? At peace? How does the lack of approval from them affect the way you love others? Now, imagine for a moment that the Creator of the universe fully approves of you. The God who knows every hair on your head. He knew you before you were born. Knows your every thought (yes, even those thoughts) and sees every time you stand up or sit down (Ps. 139). The God who knows your past and future, every sinful thought and action you've ever had or taken. The God who thinks you're so worth saving that He'd send His one and only Son to die a horrible death and take the just punishment for everything justice would demand punishment for. By your acceptance of the gift of Christ as Messiah, the price of justice is paid, and you. are. accepted. You're accepted as a child of God. Feel relieved? Free? At peace? He offers you perfect, lasting, eternal peace.

2. There are usually some unpleasant consequences to a bird landing on you, but not here. Take a moment to imagine a beautiful dove landing on you, announcing to you that peace is here, and by God's grace, through faith in Christ as your rescuer, you're fully approved. If you've accepted Him as your rescuer, each time you see a picture, card, ornament, or a live dove during Christmas, say out loud, "**I'm approved.**" See how many birds you spot.

3. Have you ever been baptized? Baptism is for those who want to publicly confess they've placed their faith in and identify with Christ's death (going underneath the water) and resurrection (coming out of the water). If you've never been baptized but have decided to place your faith in Christ, consider scheduling baptism at a local church. If you've been baptized, spend a few moments remembering it and thanking God for your new identity. If you're not ready for that step, commit to pondering the precious gift of approval. Eternal approval. When you're ready to celebrate that gift, take the plunge.

4. Are you working for approval that you can never seem to get? Meditate on these verses:

   ⁴ Now to the one who works, pay is not credited as a gift, but as something owed. ⁵ But to the one who does not work, but believes on him who declares the ungodly to be righteous, his faith is credited for righteousness (Rom. 4:4–5).

PRAYER

Lord, Your grace is amazing, and Your gifts are extravagant, thoughtful, perfect, and desperately needed. Without them, we would drown in our own plans and fleeting peace. Thank you, Lord, that You gave us Your peace. You do not give peace as the world gives it but peace that surpasses all understanding, peace that was planned since the beginning of the world, and peace that could be purchased only by our precious Savior. Help the image of the dove remind me of the approval you've so graciously and powerfully purchased for me, approval that allows me to look forward to an eternal life spent in Your magnificent presence.

Joy to the World

GIFT #4: JOY

Psalm 16:11, Isaiah 7:14, Zephaniah. 3:17, Romans 15:13, John 1:1–5,
Psalm 19:8, John 15–16 (specifically 15:9–11), 1 Peter 1:3–12,
Galatians 5:22, 2 Corinthians 1:22, Psalm 30:11–12

"Joy to the world, the Lord has come. Let Earth receive her king." Christmas songs can be comforting, fun, celebratory, and nostalgic—or hard to sing. Maybe you don't know the words. Maybe you're distracted by all that's going on around you and your to-do list—*who has time to sing*? Maybe it feels as though singing would be somehow like lying or a betrayal because the messages you're telling yourself on the inside don't match the joy and celebration of the words and melody outside. The tune of our hearts can change from moment to moment, year to year, and season to season. A moment of triumph, a year of a new relationship, a season of loss.

Have you ever sung happy words like "joy to the world" despite being sad, distressed, or in despair? The psalmists did. Every psalm is a song, and there are several called the Lament Psalms that center on sorrow and complaint (e.g., Psalms 6 and 13). The Lament Psalms are songs of faith in the darkest of circumstances. So the words "joy to the world, the Lord has come" do not mean that at the first Christmas, all who put their faith in Jesus were instantly transported to permanent glee. It's also not speaking of the latest diversion or temporary happiness. That's not worthy of "joy to the world."

No, the joy that Jesus delivers is not a weak joy that sadness, despair, or even deep, sobbing grief can choke and defeat. It's not the kind of joy that comes like a jolt of caffeine or a hometown victory. It's not even the kind of joy we try to create with our Christmas gifts to each other. No, "joy to the world" is the kind of joy that no one can wrap up except the Lord, and Christmas makes it possible. His gift of joy is unique. There's nothing like it.

This year, as you hear the Christmas songs playing
in the mall, on the radio, or even in your
head—those catchy tunes that really stick—as they deliver
short bursts of Christmas joy, consider the *deeper,
stronger, more powerful joy* made possible by Christmas
and the secret of His joy.

The Bible has a lot to say about joy. As you hear a few key, true "notes" about joy, these truths will begin to collectively harmonize. God's words about real joy are like notes that together sing of the truth of a gospel gift that cannot be drowned out, that never lies, that is never upstaged or outshined by an emotion or circumstance, a song that never gets old or outdated but invites us to dance in step with Him. His Word reveals a joy that is not only catchy, but catching; not only memorable, but lasting; not only uplifting, but a reminder that the Savior raises us up and seats us with Him (Luke 2:10, Isa. 51:11, Eph. 2:6).

Let's start with a few songs. The word *psalm* comes from the word for "to pluck or play a stringed instrument,"[1] and the psalms of the Bible are poetic songs. Psalm 16:11 NLT says, "You will show me the way of life, granting me the **joy of your presence** and the pleasures of living with you forever" (emphasis added). Psalm 9:2 NIV states, "I will be glad and **rejoice in you**; I will sing the praises of your name, O Most High" (emphasis added). That's the first and most important note of joy: **Joy comes from His Presence**. Apart from the presence of God, there is no melody, no powerful refrain, only man-made gifts that get old, break down, or get drowned out. The gift of joy *cannot* be separated from the presence of the Gift-Giver. We see evidence of that truth even with our Christmas presents to each another. Mailed gifts can be fun to open, but gifts delivered by the giver can have a more lasting, profound impact (positively or negatively). The gift isn't contained solely in the wrapping but is in the one who wrapped it.

At Christmas, we're reminded that Jesus was not only fully God, but **Immanuel**, which means "God *with* us," God *present* with us. Isaiah 7:14 explains, "Therefore the Lord himself will give you a sign: See, the virgin will conceive, have a son, and name him Immanuel." God gave Isaiah that piece of information around 700 years before the first Christmas. But were it not for Christmas, we might have a hazier view of our

Lord, the experience Isaiah would have read about: God coming as a pillar of cloud, a pillar of fire, a burning bush, and a veiled presence behind the curtain in the Holy of Holies (the unenterable part of the temple) (Exod. 13:21, 3:2–6, Lev. 16:2). With Christmas came the Savior of the world, the ultimate visual aid for our faith. He was God with us, who would show us by His **presence**—His life and His ultimate sacrifice—the preciousness of His character and depth of His love for us.

Not only do we have the record of Jesus's physical presence with us, but because of the blood Jesus shed for us, we can now be in God's presence *forever*. We can now have access to the special gospel gift of joy that comes from His presence and can rejoice in the hope of hearing His song of rejoicing over us. "The LORD your God is **with you**, the Mighty Warrior who saves. He will take great delight in you; in his love **He will no longer rebuke you, but will rejoice over you with singing**" (Zeph. 3:17 NIV, emphasis added).

The sin that separated us has been paid for and removed as far as the east is from the west. Jesus's presence with us in three acts—(1) at the first Christmas, (2) in our lives now, and (3) in its fullness in His return and our eternity—is the opera of His eternal rescue plan. The joy that He gives you to keep permanently in your heart is like the theme song for His rescue of and rejoicing over you. His plan is one that injects *permanence* into our joy because His sacrifice means we have a solid, lasting hope that one day we'll forever be in the presence of the Gift-Giver. Romans 15:13 says, "Now may the God of hope fill you with all joy and peace as you believe so that you may overflow with hope by the power of the Holy Spirit." The gospel, the good news of Jesus come to rescue us from our own noise and chaos, resonates the joy God gives you perfectly such that the song never stops. Even when the state of this fallen world seems to be drowning out this song, it still plays.

The second true note about joy is the truth about the real sources of joy on Earth during this short period while Jesus is not physically with us. While we, for now, live without Jesus's physical presence on Earth, we have at our disposal always the embodiment of our Lord in His love letter to us. John 1:1–5 says, "In the beginning was the Word, and the Word was with God, and the Word was God. He was with God in the beginning. All things were created through him, and apart from him not one thing was created that has been created. In him was life, and that life was the light of men. That light shines in the darkness, and yet the darkness did not overcome it." Therein lies the second note of joy: **Joy is found in experiencing the Word**. Jesus is the embodiment of God's Truth, the spoken, and ultimately written, Word. Jesus is the Word in the flesh. So as we read, meditate upon, and rejoice in His Word, we experience the transformation of the two-dimensional pages into our multi-dimensional heavenly

Gift-Giver. Just as sheet music is to a great song, so the words of our gift-giving God transform into experiencing the joy of His presence. Psalm 19:8 NIV says, "The **precepts of the LORD** are right, **giving joy** to the heart. The commands of the LORD are radiant, giving light to the eyes" (emphasis added). In God's Word, we have the echo and refrain of the joy of His presence, so we feed our joy with the song of His Word.

But how does that joy remain through the cacophony of confusion, grief, anxiety, and concern that are part of this broken world? We'll find our third note of joy, the answer to this question, in Jesus's comforting of His disciples. His answer is that **the faith and hope He gives you will protect, sustain, and reconnect you to your joy.** When Jesus was leaving Earth to be seated at the Father's right hand, He had to comfort the apostles, who were about to once again be without Him, a prospect causing deep grief, confusion, anxiety, and concern among them. Our grief, confusion, anxiety, and concern shake our faith, and our shaken faith interrupts the connection to the melody of our joy in Him. Jesus knew this and counseled His disciples accordingly. In John 15 and 16, Jesus counsels them (and us) on how to handle grief, confusion, anxiety, and concern. Here's what He said:

(1) **You will remain connected**: He tells them to abide in Him, stay connected with Him and His words, and follow closely to His Word and His way (John 15:1–17).

(2) **Don't be surprised by adversity:** He warns them that the world would persecute them as it persecuted Him (John 15:18–25).

(3) **Don't let adversity damage your faith, your lifeline**: "I have told you these things so that you won't abandon your faith" (John 16:1NLT).

(4) **The Holy Spirit will keep you connected (you'll hear from Jesus through Him)** (John 16:12–15).

(5) **Although they would grieve when separated from Him, they would see Him again and regain the fullness of their joy.** "Truly I tell you, you will weep and mourn, but the world will rejoice. You will become sorrowful, but your sorrow will turn to joy. When a woman is in labor, she has pain because her time has come. But when she has given birth to a child, she no longer remembers the suffering because of the joy that a person has been born into the world. So you also have sorrow now. But I will see you again. Your hearts will rejoice, and no one will take away your joy from you" (John 16:20–22).

The sweet music of the Lord's leading and encouragement beckons His followers to unwrap His gift of permanent joy. His leading is as critical to us as it was to them, for we, too, feel the ache from His absence. There will be challenges to our joy, but because of what Christ did on the cross for us, that joy cannot be completely extinguished as long as our faith is intact. In his deepest distress, Paul put it this way: "Our hearts ache, but we always have joy. We are poor, but we give spiritual riches to others. We own nothing, and yet we have everything" (2 Cor. 6:10 NLT) (see also 1 Pet. 1:6–8).

For our last three notes of joy, it's a three-part harmony. **In preparation for the ultimate, unimaginable joy of eternally being in the full presence of the Lord, God (1) prepares us, (2) fills us, and (3) dresses us up**. When He transforms us into a new creation (2 Cor. 5:17), He **prepares** us and gives us a vision and a hope for that glorious concert of joy.

> *3 Praise be to the God and Father of our Lord Jesus Christ! In his great mercy he has given us new birth into a living hope through the resurrection of Jesus Christ from the dead, 4 and into an inheritance that can never perish, spoil or fade. This inheritance is kept in heaven for you, 5 who through faith are shielded by God's power until the coming of the salvation that is ready to be revealed in the last time. 6 In all this **you greatly rejoice**, though now for a little while you may have had to suffer grief in all kinds of trials* (1 Pet. 1:3–6 NIV, emphasis added).

The Lord also **fills us** with the down payment of His presence, the source of all joy. We're filled with the Holy Spirit, and the Holy Spirit produces joy (Gal. 5:22). We're indwelled with the Holy Spirit as the down payment of the promise of being in His eternal presence (2 Cor. 1:22). We hear the truth from the Lord directly from the Spirit, remaining in His presence. Therefore, we can enjoy a lasting, surviving joy.

And God sees us as He's **dressed us with the wardrobe change paid for by the cross**: "You turned my wailing into dancing; You removed my sackcloth and clothed me with joy, that my heart may sing your praises and not be silent. LORD my God, I will praise you forever" (Ps. 30:11–12 NIV). He has covered us inside and out, dressing us up for our eternal joy.

But Jesus knew that the best way to enjoy the symphony of His joy would be to follow the Maker's instructions, to remain faithful to the One who loves you more than anyone else ever will, or can. He knew that while we're prepared in every way to experience the joy of His presence, dressed inside and out, we'd sometimes falter, trust in our own understanding instead of His (Prov. 3:5–6), and lose track of His melody. So, he tells His followers: "As the Father has loved me, so have I loved you. Remain in my love. If you keep my commands you will remain in my love, just as I have kept my Father's commands and remain in his love. **I have told you these things so that my joy may be in you and your joy may be complete**" (John 15:9–11, emphasis added).

God values our joy deeply and weeps over our grief (John 11:33–35).

Each of the Lament Psalms has at its core a familiar ring to all of us: circumstances that threaten, sometimes severely, the joy we've been given. In each, the psalmist makes a statement of faith and trust in the Lord despite his circumstances, a declaration that the psalmist won't abandon his heart song (1 Pet. 1:8–9). But what's noteworthy is that the psalmist, in the most dire, joy-threatening circumstances, practiced the Lord's presence in prayer *and* song. Although we're not meant to be fully satisfied here because we're in a broken world, not yet home in His full presence, we can still experience joy that's worthy of the title "Joy to the World."

"Joy to the World" was inspired by Psalm 98, a song that celebrates *all* that Christmas really means, from the first Christmas to our hope in Jesus now to our eternity with Him. This Christmas, dare to journey through the songs of celebration and sorrow *with Him*. Let Him give you the gift of joy, the ultimate Christmas carol.

JOY:
GIFT #4 SUMMARY AND SCRIPTURE

SUMMARY

The secret ingredient of the Lord's gift of joy is the Lord Himself—God with us, Immanuel. It's not what He can do for us or the multitude of blessings He delivers, although they are certainly good. Instead, lasting, permanent joy comes from His very presence. All the notes about joy in Scripture lead to that melodious truth. Anything that leads us closer to the Lord—whether trials (Rom. 5:3–5, Ps. 94:19), or triumphs (Neh. 8:10)—leads us closer to our soul's joy song. There will be troubles that will seek to steal our joy, but they cannot succeed in destroying it. His greatest concert is yet to come.

SCRIPTURES FOR GIFT #4

Psalm 13

[1] How long, Lord? Will you forget me forever? How long will you hide your face from me?

[2] How long will I store up anxious concerns within me, agony in my mind every day? How long will my enemy dominate me?

[3] Consider me and answer, Lord my God. Restore brightness to my eyes; otherwise, I will sleep in death.

[4] My enemy will say, "I have triumphed over him," and my foes will rejoice because I am shaken.

[5] But I have trusted in your faithful love; my heart will rejoice in your deliverance.

[6] I will sing to the Lord because he has treated me generously.

Luke 2:10 NIV

[10] But the angel said to them, "Do not be afraid. I bring you good news that will cause great joy for all the people.

Isaiah 51:11 NIV

[11] Those the Lord has rescued will return. They will enter Zion with singing; everlasting joy will crown their heads.

Gladness and joy will overtake them, and sorrow and sighing will flee away.

Ephesians 2:6 NIV

[6] And God raised us up with Christ and seated us with him in the heavenly realms in Christ Jesus,

Psalm 16:11 NIV

[11] You make known to me the path of life; you will fill me with joy in your presence, with eternal pleasures at your right hand.

Psalm 9:2 NIV

² I will be glad and rejoice in you; I will sing the praises of your name, O Most High.

Isaiah 7:14

¹⁴ Therefore, the LORD himself will give you a sign: See, the virgin will conceive, have a son, and name him Immanuel.

Leviticus 16:2

² The LORD said to Moses: "Tell your brother Aaron that he may not come whenever he wants into the holy place behind the curtain in front of the mercy seat on the ark or else he will die, because I appear in the cloud above the mercy seat.

Zephaniah 3:17 NIV

¹⁷ The LORD your God is with you, the Mighty Warrior who saves.

He will take great delight in you; in his love he will no longer rebuke you, but will rejoice over you with singing."

Romans 15:13

¹³ Now may the God of hope fill you with all joy and peace as you believe so that you may overflow with hope by the power of the Holy Spirit.

John 1:1–5

¹ In the beginning was the Word, and the Word was with God, and the Word was God. ² He was with God in the beginning. ³ All things were created through him, and apart from him not one thing was created that has been created. ⁴ In him was life, and that life was the light of men. ⁵ That light shines in the darkness, and yet the darkness did not overcome it.

Psalm 19:8 NIV

⁸ The precepts of the LORD are right, giving joy to the heart.

The commands of the LORD are radiant, giving light to the eyes.

2 Corinthians 6:9–10 NIV

⁹ [K]nown, yet regarded as unknown; dying, and yet we live on; beaten, and yet not killed; ¹⁰ sorrowful, yet always rejoicing; poor, yet making many rich; having nothing, and yet possessing everything.

1 Peter 1:6–8 NIV

⁶ In all this you greatly rejoice, though now for a little while you may have had to suffer grief in all kinds of trials. ⁷ These have come so that the proven genuineness of

your faith—of greater worth than gold, which perishes even though refined by fire—may result in praise, glory and honor when Jesus Christ is revealed. [8]Though you have not seen him, you love him; and even though you do not see him now, you believe in him and are filled with an inexpressible and glorious joy.

2 Corinthians 5:17

[17] Therefore, if anyone is in Christ, he is a new creation; the old has passed away, and see, the new has come!

1 Peter 1:3–6 NIV

[3] Praise be to the God and Father of our Lord Jesus Christ! In his great mercy he has given us new birth into a living hope through the resurrection of Jesus Christ from the dead, [4]and into an inheritance that can never perish, spoil or fade. This inheritance is kept in heaven for you, [5]who through faith are shielded by God's power until the coming of the salvation that is ready to be revealed in the last time. [6]In all this you greatly rejoice, though now for a little while you may have had to suffer grief in all kinds of trials.

Galatians 5:22–23

[22] But the fruit of the Spirit is love, joy, peace, patience, kindness, goodness, faithfulness, [23] gentleness, and self-control. The law is not against such things.

2 Corinthians 1:21–22 NIV

[21] Now it is God who makes both us and you stand firm in Christ. He anointed us, [22] set his seal of ownership on us, and put his Spirit in our hearts as a deposit, guaranteeing what is to come.

Psalm 30:11–12 NIV

[11] You turned my wailing into dancing; you removed my sackcloth and clothed me with joy, [12]that my heart may sing your praises and not be silent. Lord my God, I will praise you forever.

Proverbs 3:5–6 NIV

[5] Trust in the Lord with all your heart and lean not on your own understanding; [6]in all your ways submit to him, and he will make your paths straight.

John 15:9–11

[9] "As the Father has loved me, I have also loved you. Remain in my love. [10] If you keep my commands you will remain in my love, just as I have kept my Father's commands and remain in his love. [11] "I have told you these things so that my joy may be in you and your joy may be complete.

John 11:33–35

[33] When Jesus saw her crying, and the Jews who had come with her crying, he was deeply moved in his spirit and troubled. [34] "Where have you put him?" he asked.

"Lord," they told him, "come and see."

[35] Jesus wept.

1 Peter 1:8–9 NIV

[8] Though you have not seen him, you love him; and even though you do not see him now, you believe in him and are filled with an inexpressible and glorious joy, [9] for you are receiving the end result of your faith, the salvation of your souls.

Psalm 98 NIV

[1] Sing to the LORD a new song, for he has done marvelous things; his right hand and his holy arm have worked salvation for him. [2] The LORD has made his salvation known and revealed his righteousness to the nations. [3] He has remembered his love

and his faithfulness to Israel; all the ends of the earth have seen the salvation of our God.

[4] Shout for joy to the LORD, all the earth, burst into jubilant song with music; [5] make music to the LORD with the harp, with the harp and the sound of singing, [6] with trumpets and the blast of the ram's horn—shout for joy before the LORD, the King.

[7] Let the sea resound, and everything in it, the world, and all who live in it. [8] Let the rivers clap their hands, let the mountains sing together for joy; [9] let them sing before the LORD, for he comes to judge the earth. He will judge the world in righteousness and the peoples with equity.

JOY:
GIFT #4 REFLECTION AND PRAYER

REFLECTION QUESTIONS

1. Which note of God's song of joy do you most struggle with? Ask Him to uncover and relieve you of anything that's threatening the joy He gave you.

   a. Joy comes from His presence.

   b. Joy is found in experiencing His Word, which is the reflection of His presence.

   c. The faith and hope He gives you will protect, sustain, and reconnect you to your joy. It may be choked, but it can't be destroyed. It may be suppressed, but it can't be taken.

   d. In preparation for the ultimate, unimaginable joy of eternally being in the full presence of the Lord, God (1) prepares us with a vision and a hope, (2) fills us inside (with the Holy Spirit whose fruit includes joy), and (3) dresses us up (in clothes of righteousness, paid for by the blood of Christ).

2. **What's your favorite Christmas song?** Choose one that will remind you that a deep, strong, uncrushable joy is always available, even in the darkest places.

3. What steals your joy during the holiday season (traffic, family, lack of finances, etc.)? Meditate, replacing these joy stealers with truth, God's Word, which says: "A thief comes only to steal and kill and destroy; I have come so that they may have life and have it in abundance" (John 10:10).

4. **Practice His Presence:** Has there ever been a person you encounter all the time but haven't paid much attention to? Someone you pass every day on the way to work or when you get coffee but never acknowledge? Someone whom you may have relegated to the position of wallpaper in your life? We can treat God in the same way—as if He's just up there, somewhere, maybe distracted with important things. Or, we'll get to Him on Sunday, if at all. Our song of joy is a muffled, background noise. But in reality, God is not far away. So, what might a typical day look like if we took Him at His Word and believed this:

- In Him we live. Move. Have our being (Acts 17:26–28).
- He knows when we stand up and sit down, and He knows our every thought (Ps. 139:2).

PRAYER

Father, thank You for the glorious gift of unbeatable, unforgettable, everlasting joy. It's uniquely a gift from You that is made precious only by Your presence. As I hear happy, soulful, and nostalgic Christmas songs, remind me:

- ♪ that the joy of the words are just a shadow of the joy of Your presence.
- ♪ that their depth of emotion is just an appetizer next to the feast of the fruit of the Spirit in me.
- ♪ that as the songs bring back memories, I can also sing a song of joy for my future, for with faith in Christ comes the promise of an eternity with Immanuel.

GIFT #5: FRIENDSHIP

Malachi 1:11, Leviticus 6:15, Exodus 27:1–8, 30:1–10, Hebrews 9:1–10,
Psalm 141:2, Isaiah 55:8–9, Psalm 116:1–2, John 15:12–15, Luke 17:33,
John 16:13, 12:49, Philippians 4:18, John 12:3, Mark 15:23,
John 19:39, 2 Corinthians 2:14–15

The smells of Christmas might be a blast of familiarity for you. It could be the smell of Christmas dinner or a freshly baked dessert, a freshly cut Christmas tree, or a scented candle that lingers in the air as you decorate. Aftershave, cologne, or perfume of family members you only see once or twice a year. The smell of grandma's house. A single scent can remind you of Christmases past or memories of loved ones long gone.

Whatever the fragrance formula, it is personal
and particular. This Christmas, the scents that have
meaning for you, and even new holiday smells,
can remind you of the particular fragrance
of your personal Savior.

One word you hear around Christmastime is *frankincense*. It may be the only time you hear the word, which stems from a French word meaning high quality or *pure* incense.[1] Frankincense comes from particular plants and has been traded for thousands of years. Incense is a substance that has a particular aroma when you burn it. But frankincense is special. It's a scent all its own, and it was given a special place in God's arsenal of sensory aids to bring His creation to a greater understanding of Him.

Frankincense was the chief ingredient of the incense God required for use in the tabernacle, the original tent of worship, and later, in the temple for Israel (Exod. 30:34–38). The incense used was a unique blend to be used only where Israelites would meet with God. You could say it was God's scent, meant to remind worshippers of His name (Mal. 1:11).

When worshippers came to meet with God, they would often bring a grain offering to demonstrate their devotion to God. The grain offering was the sacrificial offering that most closely resembled giving presents to the Lord. A portion of the flour and oil of the offering was burned as a memorial portion, which was set aside as a remembrance for worshippers to *remember* what the Lord had forgiven them of or done for them. Importantly, the memorial portion was to be burned with pure incense as "an aroma pleasing to the LORD" (Lev. 6:15), and this sweet smell would help the worshipper forever associate with the grace and gifts the Lord had bestowed. The worshipper's gift was in part a gift given to remember gifts received.

But that memorial portion was burned in the *outer* courtyard of the tabernacle, the early temple where the Israelites worshipped (Exod. 27:1–8). *Inside* the tabernacle, where the worshipper would meet with God, was a second altar called the altar of incense, otherwise known as the golden altar of incense because it was covered with pure gold. This second altar was tactically placed in the holy place, the main worship area inside the tabernacle. It was literally much closer to the Lord because it was closer to the final enclosed cell of the tabernacle called the Holy of Holies where He would be present, separated by a curtain or veil between the Holy of Holies and the main part of the tabernacle called the Holy Place (Exod. 30:1–10, Heb. 9:1–10). The incense burned on the golden altar of incense caused the distinctive fragrance to give the tabernacle a distinctive aroma. As a worshipper entered the holy place of the tabernacle or temple, there would be no mistaking the sweet aroma of pure incense—likely a very welcome change from the stench of blood sacrifices taking place outside at the bronze altar. You might imagine the smell of an unrefrigerated butcher shop being replaced by the fragrance of a perfumery or the intensified smell of freshly cut trees or plants.

What a relief it must have been to exchange those smells. The relief of coming closer to His presence, coming inside from the weather, and coming from the stench of the blood sacrifices for sin, and the ugliness of the death-wages of sin, into the welcoming fragrance of forgiveness and fellowship with the Lord. They could complete their obedience to God's commands, the required sacrifices of a righteous and just God, outside the tent, and come into the tent for voluntary worship—to enjoy and celebrate the gift of grace in sweet scents.

It was such a sweet aroma and so associated with communing with God that the pure incense burning on the golden altar came to represent pure-hearted prayers of God's people wafting up to Him (Ps. 141:2). The ultimate act of friendship and fellowship with God was found in the people's desire (1) to be near Him in the tent of meeting and

(2) to commune with Him in the prayers of their forgiven and grateful hearts. Prayer is the ultimate expression of the gift, the offering, fellowship, and friendship with God.

The aroma of prayer can become the familiar scent of a trusted friend. The very idea that the God of the universe, the One and Only, gives us access to His ear is a miracle of friendship. We mostly extend our friendship to those around us that are just like us, or at least with whom we have something in common. We befriend someone we think is our equal, with whom we can exchange value—I can do something for you, and you can do something for me. I like doing this stuff, and you do, too. But to have God's ear, to have His friendship, is spectacularly more generous. The ear of God, for whom we can do nothing (John 15:5). The ear of God, whose thoughts and ways are not our thoughts and ways (Isa. 55:8). The ear of God, who has no equal (Isa. 40:12–31). That *He* would stoop to hear us is friendship above and beyond. The psalmist said it perfectly: "I love the Lord, for He heard my voice; he heard my cry for mercy. Because He turned his ear to me, I will call on Him as long as I live" (Ps. 116:1–2 NIV).

And then on top of His stooping to *hear us*, His communication with us is two-way. He speaks to us. The fact that He tells us His plans in His Word and through the Holy Spirit is nothing short of amazing grace. If you've ever been put in charge of organizing an event or project, you know that sharing your plans with anyone but your closest confidants isn't easy. You open yourself up to people's opinions and second-guessing. But the God of the universe sacrificed His own perfect Son to pay for our sins so we could have fellowship with Him and He could share His ultimate plan to redeem humanity with us.

Jesus expressed His gospel gift of friendship this way: "This is my command: Love one another as I have loved you. No one has greater love than this: to lay down his life for his friends. You are my friends if you do what I command you. I do not call you servants anymore, because a servant doesn't know what his master is doing. I have called you friends, because I have made known to you everything I have heard from my Father" (John 15:12–15). Jesus defined those to whom He offered His friendship as those with whom He shares His Father's words, God's most intimate whisperings. He not only hears us, but He speaks to us. He not only speaks to us, but He speaks the precious, intimate words of the Father. He gives us the very best words. True words. Powerful words. Compassionate words. Encouraging words. Correcting words. Directing words. Loving words. Our Father's words.

But Jesus also had something to say about how we can know whether we are His friends. Put simply, Jesus said we are His friends when we love like He loves us. How is that? With a lay-down-your-life love. When we love with a lay-down-your-life love, it becomes evident that we're in tight with Jesus. We're buds. We hang out. Because it's only with the gifts He gives us that we're able to love like that. It's because He laid down *His* life for us that we can lay down ours for others. When we love like that, it's only because we've been loved like that. When we love like that, it's only because we've fully received the extravagant beauty and sacrifice of the perfect life Jesus lived and gave up in a horrifically painful death. When we know we're loved like that, really loved like that, we're free to give away what we have—there's so much to distribute.

Our friend Jesus wants desperately for us to love with a lay-down-your-life love because He knows that when you spend your life extravagantly, you *save* it, making it purposeful and fruitful (Luke 17:33). The sweet aroma of our friendship is picked up when we listen to the Word and the Holy Spirit (John 16:13, 12:49); share our deepest thoughts and feelings, fears, and triumphs with the Lord; and let the overflow of His words poured into us spill out, a shared fragrance.

When the stench of our sin threatens the sweet aroma of fellowship with the Lord, He's faithful to restore the sweet smell if we'll just offer up that sin in a prayer of confession, and let him destroy the sin before it destroys us. The same contrasting sin-sacrifice stench and sweet smell of incense for the Israelite worshipper are the olfactory swings of our lifelong walk with the Lord.

But Jesus made it possible for us to live in the sweet scent of the Lord's presence now and forever. He *was* and *is* the permanent, fragrant offering of incense on the golden altar (Phil. 4:18). He was the memorial portion whose broken body we remember at communion in remembrance of Him and what He did for us.

From the first Christmas to the first Easter, His offering of Himself as the sweet aroma pleasing to the Lord was illustrated. Upon hearing of Jesus's birth, the magi brought Him gifts of gold, frankincense, and myrrh. The pure perfume of the frankincense and myrrh was only a down payment, a symbol of the fragrant offering His life and sacrifice would become on the most valuable altar—that of gold, the altar closest to God's presence. During His ministry on Earth, Mary poured expensive perfume on Jesus's feet, and the house "filled with the fragrance" (John 12:3). Finally, at His death, Jesus was offered the sweet smelling myrrh to drink before he was crucified (Mark 15:23), and His body was wrapped in 75 pounds of a myrrh mixture (John 19:39). Myrrh was an ingestible form of perfume and incense.

You only learn the smells of the people you're really close to—the sweet smells, and the not so sweet. While we recognize the voice and the face of many a stranger, the smell of a friend's perfume or cologne may be recognizable only by those who know it best. How well do you know the sweet aroma of Christ? Drawing near to Him in fellowship, in the gift of friendship He offers, we can begin to recognize the preferable scent of His presence in the practice of prayer.

What's more, God's plan is that through us, he spreads the fragrance of Christ everywhere. Second Corinthians 2:14–15 NIV puts it this way: "But thanks be to God, who always leads us as captives in Christ's triumphal procession and uses us to spread the aroma of the knowledge of him everywhere. For we are to God the pleasing aroma of Christ among those who are being saved and those who are perishing." We are to "walk in the way of love, just as Christ loved us and gave himself up for us as a fragrant offering" (Eph. 5:2 NIV).

May the gift of love to others that we give this Christmas be like the Lord's Christmas gift of Himself—"a fragrant offering."

FRIENDSHIP:
GIFT #5 SUMMARY AND SCRIPTURE

SUMMARY

God's scent, from the tabernacle to the tomb, was the same: sweet. Frankincense and myrrh were present at His birthday celebration with the wise men, and myrrh at his burial. In between, costly perfume was poured on Him. While these pure, sweet scents were applied liberally to Jesus throughout His earthbound life, from Christmas to Easter they were just a reminder, or symbol, of Jesus's role as the sweet-smelling aroma of the Lord. We only experience that sweet scent as we draw close to Him in fellowship and friendship. Only those closest to you know your best smells (and your worst), and we are overwhelmingly blessed with the opportunity to become familiar with the sweet scent of the King of the universe. He stoops to listen to us, powerfully speaks to us and through us, and paid the price for our sins on the cross so a holy, perfect, sinless God of sweet purity could fellowship with us, commune with us, and be close to us forever.

SCRIPTURES FOR GIFT #5

Malachi 1:11

[11] "My name will be great among the nations, from the rising of the sun to its setting. Incense and pure offerings will be presented in my name in every place because my name will be great among the nations," says the LORD of Armies.

Leviticus 6:15

[15] The priest is to remove a handful of fine flour and olive oil from the grain offering, with all the frankincense that is on the offering, and burn its memorial portion on the altar as a pleasing aroma to the LORD.

Exodus 27:1–8

[1] "You are to construct the altar of acacia wood. The altar must be square, 7½ feet long, and 7½ feet wide; it must be 4½ feet high. [2] Make horns for it on its four corners; the horns are to be of one piece. Overlay it with bronze. [3] Make its pots for removing ashes, and its shovels, basins, meat forks, and firepans; make all its utensils of bronze. [4] Construct a grate for it of bronze mesh, and make four bronze rings on the mesh at its four corners. [5] Set it below, under the altar's ledge, so that the mesh comes halfway up the altar. [6] Then make poles for the altar, poles of acacia wood, and overlay them with bronze. [7] The poles are to be inserted into the rings so that the poles are on two sides of the altar when it is carried. [8] Construct the altar with boards so that it is hollow. They are to make it just as it was shown to you on the mountain.

Exodus 30:1–10

[1] "You are to make an altar for the burning of incense; make it of acacia wood. [2] It must be square, eighteen inches long and eighteen inches wide; it must be thirty-six inches high. Its horns must be of one piece with it. [3] Overlay its top, all around its sides, and its horns with pure gold; make a gold molding all around it. [4] Make two gold rings for it under the molding on two of its sides; put these on opposite sides of it to be holders for the poles to carry it with. [5] Make the poles of acacia wood and overlay them with gold.

[6] "You are to place the altar in front of the curtain by the ark of the testimony—in front of the mercy seat that is over the testimony—where I will meet with you. [7] Aaron must burn fragrant incense on it; he must burn it every morning when he tends the lamps. [8] When Aaron sets up the lamps at twilight, he must burn incense. There is to be an incense offering before the LORD throughout your generations. [9] You must not offer unauthorized incense on it, or a burnt or grain offering; you are not to pour a drink offering on it.

[10] "Once a year Aaron is to perform the atonement ceremony for the altar. Throughout your generations he is to perform the atonement ceremony for it once a year, with the blood of the sin offering for atonement on the horns. The altar is especially holy to the LORD."

Hebrews 9:1–10

[1] Now the first covenant also had regulations for ministry and an earthly sanctuary. [2] For a tabernacle was set up, and in the first room, which is called the holy place, were the lampstand, the table, and the presentation loaves. [3] Behind the second curtain was a tent called the most holy place. [4] It had the gold altar of incense and the ark of the covenant, covered with gold on all sides, in which was a gold jar containing the manna, Aaron's staff that budded, and the tablets of the covenant. [5] The cherubim of glory were above the ark overshadowing the mercy seat. It is not possible to speak about these things in detail right now.

[6] With these things prepared like this, the priests enter the first room repeatedly, performing their ministry. [7] But the high priest alone enters the second room, and he does that only once a year, and never without blood, which he offers for himself and for the sins the people had committed in ignorance. [8] The Holy Spirit was making it clear that the way into the most holy place had not yet been disclosed while the first tabernacle was still standing. [9] This is a symbol for the present time, during which gifts and sacrifices are offered that cannot perfect the worshiper's conscience. [10] They are physical regulations and only deal with food, drink, and various washings imposed until the time of the new order.

Psalm 141:2 NIV

² May my prayer be set before you like incense; may the lifting up of my hands be like the evening sacrifice

John 15:5 NIV

⁵ "I am the vine; you are the branches. If you remain in me and I in you, you will bear much fruit; apart from me you can do nothing.

Isaiah 55:8

⁸ "For my thoughts are not your thoughts, and your ways are not my ways." This is the LORD's declaration.

Isaiah 40:12–31

¹² Who has measured the waters in the hollow of his hand or marked off the heavens with the span of his hand? Who has gathered the dust of the earth in a measure or weighed the mountains on a balance and the hills on the scales? ¹³ Who has directed the Spirit of the LORD, or who gave him counsel? ¹⁴ Who did he consult? Who gave him understanding and taught him the paths of justice? Who taught him knowledge and showed him the way of understanding?

¹⁵ Look, the nations are like a drop in a bucket; they are considered as a speck of dust on the scales; he lifts up the islands like fine dust. ¹⁶ Lebanon's cedars are not enough for fuel, or its animals enough for a burnt offering.

¹⁷ All the nations are as nothing before him; they are considered by him as empty nothingness. ¹⁸ With whom will you compare God? What likeness will you set up for comparison with him? ¹⁹ An idol?—something that a smelter casts and a metalworker plates with gold and makes silver chains for? ²⁰ A poor person contributes wood for a pedestal that will not rot.

He looks for a skilled craftsman to set up an idol that will not fall over. ²¹ Do you not know? Have you not heard? Has it not been declared to you from the beginning? Have you not considered the foundations of the earth? ²² God is enthroned above the circle of the earth; its inhabitants are like grasshoppers. He stretches out the heavens like thin cloth and spreads them out like a tent to live in. ²³ He reduces princes to nothing and makes judges of the earth like a wasteland. ²⁴ They are barely planted, barely sown, their stem hardly takes root in the ground when he blows on them and they wither, and a whirlwind carries them away like stubble.

²⁵ "To whom will you compare me, or who is my equal?" asks the Holy One. ²⁶ Look up and see! Who created these? He brings out the stars by number; he calls all of them by name. Because of his great power and strength, not one of them is missing.

²⁷ Jacob, why do you say, and, Israel, why do you assert: "My way is hidden from the Lord, and my claim is ignored by my God"? ²⁸ Do you not know? Have you not heard? The Lord is the everlasting God, the Creator of the whole earth. He never becomes faint or weary; there is no limit to his understanding. ²⁹ He gives strength to the faint and strengthens the powerless.

³⁰ Youths may become faint and weary, and young men stumble and fall, ³¹ but those who trust in the Lord will renew their strength; they will soar on wings like eagles; they will run and not become weary, they will walk and not faint

Psalm 116:1–2 NIV

¹ I love the Lord, for he heard my voice; he heard my cry for mercy. ² Because he turned his ear to me, I will call on him as long as I live.

John 15:12–15

¹² "This is my command: Love one another as I have loved you. ¹³ No one has greater love than this: to lay down his life for his friends. ¹⁴ You are my friends if you do what I command you. ¹⁵ I do not call you servants anymore, because a servant doesn't know what his master is doing. I have called you friends, because I have made known to you everything I have heard from my Father.

Luke 17:33

³³ Whoever tries to make his life secure will lose it, and whoever loses his life will preserve it.

John 16:13

¹³ When the Spirit of truth comes, he will guide you into all the truth. For he will not speak on his own, but he will speak whatever he hears. He will also declare to you what is to come.

Psalm 25:14 NIV

¹⁴ The Lord confides in those who fear him; he makes his covenant known to them.

John 12:49

⁴⁹ For I have not spoken on my own, but the Father himself who sent me has given me a command to say everything I have said.

John 12:3 NIV

³ Then Mary took about a pint of pure nard, an expensive perfume; she poured it on Jesus' feet and wiped his feet with her hair. And the house was filled with the fragrance of the perfume.

Mark 15:23

²³ They tried to give him wine mixed with myrrh, but he did not take it.

John 19:39

³⁹ Nicodemus (who had previously come to him at night) also came, bringing a mixture of about seventy-five pounds of myrrh and aloes.

2 Corinthians 2:14–15 NIV

¹⁴ But thanks be to God, who always leads us as captives in Christ's triumphal procession and uses us to spread the aroma of the knowledge of him everywhere. ¹⁵ For we are to God the pleasing aroma of Christ among those who are being saved and those who are perishing.

Ephesians 5:2 NIV

² And walk in the way of love, just as Christ loved us and gave himself up for us as a fragrant offering and sacrifice to God.

Philippians 4:18 NIV

¹⁸ I have received full payment and have more than enough. I am amply supplied, now that I have received from Epaphroditus the gifts you sent. They are a fragrant offering, an acceptable sacrifice, pleasing to God.

FRIENDSHIP:
GIFT #5 REFLECTION AND PRAYER

REFLECTION QUESTIONS

1. Is there a smell or smells that you associate with Christmas? Someone's cooking? The smell of Grandma's house? A Christmas candle? What associations or thoughts does that smell(s) bring up for you?

2. Imagine if there were a perfectly pure, sweet smell you could readily identify as the Lord's scent. Every time you were near Him, in His presence, it wafted into your nostrils. How might that change how you feel, think, or act in the moment you picked up that scent?

3. If you had a best friend or loved one with a signature scent you could always recognize, how do you think you would react when you smelled that smell?

4. Do you find it hard to believe that the Lord is your *friend*? To believe He is truly your friend, what do you need to adjust about how you think about the Lord?

5. Consider preparing a gift for the Lord that is a reminder, memorial, or remembrance of gifts *He* has given *you*. It could be a picture, an object, a song or a poem, a gesture or a gift to others, a specific time with Him in thanks, a decoration, a sign, and so on. Just something that reminds you of what He's given you: a friend, a family, freedom, peace, eternity with Him. There are too many to mention. For example, you might give a gift to an organization that gives out God's Word in remembrance of that gift to you. You might put a picture of your whole family inside the front cover of a Bible and give it away to family members in remembrance that they were God's gift to you.

PRAYER

Father, remind us that we need never be lonely with Your mighty hand of friendship extended through Your Son's life sacrifice. You are always present and available because His sacrifice removed the barrier between us. Although we bear Your image, we don't naturally share Your thoughts or ways, yet you stoop to hear us. We don't readily listen and often don't follow your pure, perfect, preserving words, yet you share Your plans with us. Let Your lay-down-your-life love invade our every thought and action such that we love others as You do and prove ourselves your friends. Let the aroma of our lives smell like Your scent.

GIFT #6: PROVISION

John 6, 20:30–31, Psalm 104:14, Matthew 26:26, 1 Corinthians 11:23–24

What would a Christmas celebration be without baked goods or tasty treats? All over the world, Christmas is celebrated with goodies of all kinds: breads, rolls, cakes, pastries, fruits, nuts, candy, and even fish. On the other end of the spectrum, Christmas evokes images of soup lines and humble homeless shelter feasts. From feast to famine. The first Christmas more closely resembled the latter. A humble birth in a humble manger.

During Jesus's earthly stint, however, the two ends of the spectrum met: feast met famine for more than 5,000 men, which meant that with women and children, there were likely at least twice, if not three times that number. Truly, it was a mass of humanity that Jesus fed with only a few loaves and fish, along with a blessing. He provided a feast where there was only a little boy's generosity giving up his lunch in hopes it would provide for others.

As you enjoy the holiday high-carb diet or
a humble meal, savor not only the provision
you're chewing but the *Christmas gift of God's eternal,
abundant provision*. Celebrate God bursting into
our broken world to show us His provision and
show Himself the ultimate, eternal Provider:

John relays the scene: thousands followed Jesus because they had seen Him heal the sick. They had hope because He had power—power over sickness and power over death. But when thousands of tummies grumbled, the disciples, who saw and knew Jesus's power, could not imagine Jesus as Provider. They failed that test of faith. His disciples could not imagine Jesus feeding the whole crowd because it would cost a fortune—more than half a year's wages, which they didn't have. Not only did they not see Jesus as Provider, but they did not see him as Creator. When a boy offered his lunch of five loaves and two fish, they could not understand how Jesus would *create* mountainous meals out of a modest lunch.

Jesus understood that it was not the provision they failed to have faith in, but the Provider. An overlooked, but very important, part of John's recounting of the thousands being fed is found in John 6:11 NASB. Depending on the translation, it may appear in only three tiny words: "Jesus took the loaves, and **having given thanks**, He distributed to those who were seated" (emphasis added).

"Having given thanks" would almost certainly have been Jesus praying over the bread (and fish) as faithful Jewish people of the time would, praying a prayer called the *Hamotzi* ("who brings forth"): **"Blessed are You, Lord, Our God, King of the Universe, who brings forth bread from the *earth*"** (emphasis added). Some Hebrew translations say **"who brings forth bread from *heaven*."** It was the customary biblical prayer of Jewish history, spoken even today, derived from Psalm 104:14.

Jesus was not making the bread or the fish *holy* with the Hamotzi prayer. No. He was *blessing Father God*, the first person of the Trinity, for the provision, recognizing that all provision comes from Him. He prayed, thanking the Provider *before* the bread and fish were multiplied. He was not making holy bread and holy fish. He was declaring the Provider of the fish and bread holy. As a word of caution, this passage is not teaching that God makes those with faith wealthy with stuff. Rather, it is all about the One in whom we can have faith for the provision.

The word *provide* comes from the Latin word that means "to see before," or to foresee and attend to.[3] God is the only One who can **see beforehand and provide accordingly**. He saw His Son preaching to thousands, He saw the thousands listening, and He knew that what they needed *most* was to *believe*. Their eternity depended on it, as did the billions of people He knew would hear and read and recount what happened over the years to come. The dominance of oral tradition around the world means that even more than three and a half **billion** copies of the Bible sold, which contain this account of a miraculous meal, are only a **small portion** of the number of people who were provided for that day. John said of these recorded miracles: "Jesus performed many other signs in the presence of his disciples that are not written in this book. [31] But these are written so that you may believe that Jesus is the Messiah, the Son of God, and that by believing you may have life in his name" (John 20:30–31). God provided not only the fish and loaves but the story of this provision to many billions of people and counting so they would believe in their Savior and have *life*. Eternal life.

God is the only One who could see ahead—all the way ahead—to eternity. Put another way, God's provision is what we would provide if we had unlimited power and knew all that God knows.

The throng of thousands that got the free fish and loaf dinner, however, like us, had some significant visual impairment.

After this wonder-filled feast, every one of the 12 disciples picked up a full basket of leftovers to keep as a sort of divine doggie bag, and no doubt as a reminder of the thoughtful, gracious, perfect Provider they had in the Lord. But after the cleanup, the people wanted more bread. They followed the free meal to Capernaum. They travelled by boat. Jesus travelled by water-walking. Baffled by His quick commute, the crowds demanded a repeat performance of God-sized proportions. They wanted manna, heavenly bread, to fall from the sky as it had when God had Moses in charge.

They could only see ahead to the next meal. At best, they could see ahead to the span of their lives on Earth, thinking of how to make that relative blip of time most comfortable, most survivable. Their visual impairment did not let them see the abundant provision that was right in front of them and far, far greater than any dinner could ever be. They could not see right in front of them, and they could not see into eternity. As Jesus told them, He was the Bread of Life—the **provision**, the sustenance, the survival supply for real, eternal life: "Truly I tell you, anyone who believes has eternal life. I am the bread of life" (John 6:47–48).

You see, when Jesus prayed the *Hamotzi* prayer, He had clear and perfect vision—pro vision of the Provider and the eternal Provision. When Jesus prayed, **"Blessed are You, Lord, Our God, King of the Universe, Who brings forth bread from the earth [or heaven],"** He knew that *He Himself* was the one God brought forth from heaven, the true manna **from heaven**. He knew that *He Himself* was the one God would bring forth, resurrected **from inside the earth**. He knew that His body would be broken to pay for the sins of a broken world, and that forevermore His followers would worship Him in communion, breaking bread in remembrance of Him. At the last supper, a Passover meal, Jesus forever cemented the understanding that He *is* the sustenance of life: "While they were eating, Jesus took bread, and when he had given thanks, he broke it and gave it to his disciples, saying, 'Take and eat; this is my body'" (Matt. 26:26 NIV) (see also 1 Cor. 11:23–24). At every Sabbath meal, the bread would be broken and distributed carefully and reverently, as it still is today. Among Christ-followers, we call this communion. Communion is a time when we remember that His body was broken for our sustenance, our eternal supply and survival, our eternal life, our eternal *provision*—the supply from the One who could see ahead to what we need.

In this season of celebration, we can be short-sighted or totally blind in much the same way as the well-fed throngs. We, too, may find ourselves following Jesus, looking for a free meal or bigger baskets of bread. We, too, may look myopically at only the circumstances right in front of us—the broken condition of the world—and have our faith shaken in His provision because we've not gotten what we hoped for or expected. We might look at the circumstances before us, not seeing the lifelong, satisfying provision that is Jesus Christ. Our vision ahead to the eternal life Jesus paid for us to have is perhaps most clouded by the poverty and suffering in the present world. It was for those suffering people, most of all, that Jesus came and gave His very life so that their suffering would be only for the span of this life spent in our broken world.

You might identify with Mary and Joseph's provision problem in Bethlehem. As they entered the city for the government census, finding no place to stay, perhaps they, too, looked at their circumstances and wondered about God's provision. After all, Mary was carrying the Son of God; couldn't He spare a bed? They may have wondered if God was with them, God as *provider*. Yet, in the humble beginnings of the manger, the King of the universe was born. Every promise He made began to unfold. The richest provision, the greatest lasting treasure, was there in the hay. He came and lived a life identifying Himself with the poorest and most humble. And He came for all of us, as all of us are provision-challenged, unable to provide for ourselves what we most need for an eternal journey.

If maybe you've been following Jesus for just short-term provisions and the stuff of unsatisfying meals, take Jesus's advice this Christmas about what's worth working for:

> [26] *Jesus answered, "Truly I tell you, you are looking for me, not because you saw the signs, but because you ate the loaves and were filled.* [27] *Don't work for the food that perishes but for the food that lasts for eternal life, which the Son of Man will give you, because God the Father has set his seal of approval on him."* [28] *"What can we do to perform the works of God?" they asked.* [29] *Jesus replied, "This is the work of God—that you **believe** in the one he has sent"* (John 6:26–29, emphasis added).

PROVISION:
GIFT #6 SUMMARY AND SCRIPTURES

SUMMARY

God's gift of provision can take many forms. He certainly provides our daily bread. There's nothing wrong with praying thanks and praise to the God who gives us what we need each day to survive or thrive in our temporary home. But His provision is far richer than we know or recognize. His greatest provision came in the package delivered to a humble manger from heaven. We underestimate the value and necessity of His provision because we simply can't see clearly (we have no vision of what we need most for an eternity). We have no provision apart from Him. We don't know best what we need to pack for that long of a journey. In the short blip that is this earthly life, many in this broken world suffer poverty, hunger, want. But Christ came that the poor, the brokenhearted, the cast-down would have hope and hope eternal—hope in the eternal provision of an eternal life hidden and protected by Christ Himself.

SCRIPTURES FOR GIFT #6

John 6:11 NASB
[11] Jesus then took the loaves, and having given thanks, He distributed to those who were seated; likewise also of the fish as much as they wanted.

Psalm 104:14
[14] He causes grass to grow for the livestock and provides crops for man to cultivate, producing food from the earth.

John 20:30–31
[30] Jesus performed many other signs in the presence of his disciples that are not written in this book. [31] But these are written so that you may believe that Jesus is the Messiah, the Son of God, and that by believing you may have life in his name.

John 6:47–48
[47] "Truly I tell you, anyone who believes has eternal life. [48] I am the bread of life."

Matthew 26:26 NIV
[26] While they were eating, Jesus took bread, and when he had given thanks, he broke it and gave it to his disciples, saying, "Take and eat; this is my body."

1 Corinthians 11:23–24
[23] For I received from the Lord what I also passed on to you: On the night when he was betrayed, the Lord Jesus took bread, [24] and when he had given thanks, broke it, and said, "This is my body, which is for you. Do this in remembrance of me."

John 6:1–58

[1] After this, Jesus crossed the Sea of Galilee (or Tiberias). [2] A huge crowd was following him because they saw the signs that he was performing by healing the sick. [3] Jesus went up a mountain and sat down there with his disciples.

[4] Now the Passover, a Jewish festival, was near. [5] So when Jesus looked up and noticed a huge crowd coming toward him, he asked Philip, "Where will we buy bread so that these people can eat?" [6] He asked this to test him, for he himself knew what he was going to do.

[7] Philip answered him, "Two hundred denarii worth of bread wouldn't be enough for each of them to have a little."

[8] One of his disciples, Andrew, Simon Peter's brother, said to him, [9] "There's a boy here who has five barley loaves and two fish—but what are they for so many?"

[10] Jesus said, "Have the people sit down."

There was plenty of grass in that place; so they sat down. The men numbered about five thousand. [11] Then Jesus took the loaves, and after giving thanks he distributed them to those who were seated—so also with the fish, as much as they wanted.

[12] When they were full, he told his disciples, "Collect the leftovers so that nothing is wasted." [13] So they collected them and filled twelve baskets with the pieces from the five barley loaves that were left over by those who had eaten.

[14] When the people saw the sign he had done, they said, "This truly is the Prophet who is to come into the world."

[15] Therefore, when Jesus realized that they were about to come and take him by force to make him king, he withdrew again to the mountain by himself.

[16] When evening came, his disciples went down to the sea, [17] got into a boat, and started across the sea to Capernaum. Darkness had already set in, but Jesus had not yet come to them. [18] A high wind arose, and the sea began to churn. [19] After they had rowed about three or four miles, they saw Jesus walking on the sea. He was coming near the boat, and they were afraid. [20] But he said to them, "It is I. Don't be afraid." [21] Then they were willing to take him on board, and at once the boat was at the shore where they were heading.

[22] The next day, the crowd that had stayed on the other side of the sea saw there had been only one boat. They also saw that Jesus had not boarded the boat with his disciples, but that his disciples had gone off alone. [23] Some boats from Tiberias came near the place where they had eaten the bread after the Lord had given thanks. [24] When the crowd saw that neither Jesus nor his disciples were there, they got into the boats and went to Capernaum looking for Jesus. [25] When they found him on the other side of the sea, they said to him, "Rabbi, when did you get here?"

²⁶ Jesus answered, "Truly I tell you, you are looking for me, not because you saw the signs, but because you ate the loaves and were filled. ²⁷ Don't work for the food that perishes but for the food that lasts for eternal life, which the Son of Man will give you, because God the Father has set his seal of approval on him."

²⁸ "What can we do to perform the works of God?" they asked.

²⁹ Jesus replied, "This is the work of God—that you believe in the one he has sent."

³⁰ "What sign, then, are you going to do so we may see and believe you?" they asked. "What are you going to perform? ³¹ Our ancestors ate the manna in the wilderness, just as it is written: **He gave them bread from heaven to eat.**"

³² Jesus said to them, "Truly I tell you, Moses didn't give you the bread from heaven, but my Father gives you the true bread from heaven. ³³ For the bread of God is the one who comes down from heaven and gives life to the world."

³⁴ Then they said, "Sir, give us this bread always."

³⁵ "I am the bread of life," Jesus told them. "No one who comes to me will ever be hungry, and no one who believes in me will ever be thirsty again. ³⁶ But as I told you, you've seen me, and yet you do not believe. ³⁷ Everyone the Father gives me will come to me, and the one who comes to me I will never cast out. ³⁸ For I have come down from heaven, not to do my own will, but the will of him who sent me. ³⁹ This is the will of him who sent me: that I should lose none of those he has given me but should raise them up on the last day. ⁴⁰ For this is the will of my Father: that everyone who sees the Son and believes in him will have eternal life, and I will raise him up on the last day."

⁴¹ Therefore the Jews started complaining about him because he said, "I am the bread that came down from heaven." ⁴² They were saying, "Isn't this Jesus the son of Joseph, whose father and mother we know? How can he now say, 'I have come down from heaven'?"

⁴³ Jesus answered them, "Stop complaining among yourselves. ⁴⁴ No one can come to me unless the Father who sent me draws him, and I will raise him up on the last day. ⁴⁵ It is written in the Prophets: **And they will all be taught by God.** Everyone who has listened to and learned from the Father comes to me— ⁴⁶ not that anyone has seen the Father except the one who is from God. He has seen the Father.

⁴⁷ "Truly I tell you, anyone who believes has eternal life. ⁴⁸ I am the bread of life. ⁴⁹ Your ancestors ate the manna in the wilderness, and they died. ⁵⁰ This is the bread that comes down from heaven so that anyone may eat of it and not die. ⁵¹ I am the living bread that came down from heaven. If anyone eats of this bread he will live forever. The bread that I will give for the life of the world is my flesh."

⁵² At that, the Jews argued among themselves, "How can this man give us his flesh to eat?"

[53] So Jesus said to them, "Truly I tell you, unless you eat the flesh of the Son of Man and drink his blood, you do not have life in yourselves. [54] The one who eats my flesh and drinks my blood has eternal life, and I will raise him up on the last day, [55] because my flesh is true food and my blood is true drink. [56] The one who eats my flesh and drinks my blood remains in me, and I in him. [57] Just as the living Father sent me and I live because of the Father, so the one who feeds on me will live because of me. [58] This is the bread that came down from heaven; it is not like the manna your ancestors ate—and they died. The one who eats this bread will live forever."

PROVISION:
GIFT #6 REFLECTION AND PRAYER

REFLECTION QUESTIONS

1. Find an opportunity this Christmas season to have a meal in which you "break bread" with others, with the focus of the meal being to give thanks for the Lord (sort of a Thanksgiving 2.0). If you're on your own this Christmas, find someone, or many someones, who don't have much bread, and bring them some as a thank you to the Lord for the life (for eternity) that He's purchased and provided for you.

2. Christmas can be a baked-goods bonanza, but consider picking a day or a time when you'll fast from baked goods and trade in the cookie or muffin for a few moments of communion with the Lord. Spend a few moments meditating on how He is far sweeter, His satisfaction much longer, and His promises far more rejuvenating to our soul. Pick one or two verses that are favorites for you and make them a meal. For little ones, you might write down a verse for them or have them write it down, and pack it with their sweet treats. My personal favorite is Psalm 34:8 NLT: "Taste and see that the LORD is good. Oh, the joys of those who take refuge in him!"

3. Trust in His provision. Do you struggle with the idea that God will provide for you? Do you trust in His eternal X-ray vision to know what your future holds and what you need for the journey? Read Psalm 139. Ask God to help you *believe* Psalm 139.

PRAYER

Lord Jesus, forgive me if I've been believing that I sustain *myself*, that real provision can be bought online, or that You are not the provision or the provider. Bring me into the light of Your Word that is a flashlight for my feet and gives me full sight of your eternal perspective so I can see what a miraculous provision You are for me. As I enjoy cakes, bread, candy, cookies, and the trimmings and trappings of the provision for daily life, bring to my heart and mind the reminder that You are the only sustenance that loves me, the only sustaining source that fully satisfies.

GIFT #7: MERCY

Luke 2:8–20, Revelation 5:11, Matthew 18:10, Hebrews 9:4–5, Exodus 25:22,
Isaiah 37:16, Psalm 99:1, Leviticus 16:11–15, Romans 3:25–26, Genesis 3:24,
Exodus 26:1, 31–33, Exodus 33:20, Romans 3:23, Isaiah 55:1–3, 6–13,
2 Corinthians 1:3, James 5:11, 1 Peter 2:10, Mark 5:19, Philippians 2:27,
Luke 18:13, 1 Timothy 1:13, Luke 6:36, Romans 12:1, Lamentations 3:22–23

Angels are not like cute ornaments or unicorns. No, every time someone sees one, their reaction is to be terrified. We know that because the angel inevitably has to say, "Don't be afraid." Perhaps one of the best examples is Jesus's birth announcement, the first Christmas (Luke 2:8–20). Some shepherds were in the fields, minding their own business—literally—when an angel of the Lord appeared and said, "Do not be afraid. I bring you good news that will cause great joy for all the people" (Luke 2:10 NIV). You can imagine the shepherds catching their breath at the sight of God's glory all around the announcing angel. The angel went on, "Today in the town of David a Savior has been born to you; he is the Messiah, the Lord. This will be a sign to you: You will find a baby wrapped in clothes and lying in a manger" (Luke 2:11–12 NIV). At that moment, BAM! An *army* of angels appeared. Instantly reporting for duty. No self-respecting, let alone God-respecting angel would miss participating in the announcement of their commander-in-chief arriving on Earth to execute the plan of all time, the rescue operation of all rescue operations, the eternity-saving mission.

This first Christmas parade involved an army of seemingly massive scale. When the heavenly host of angels were heard to praise Jesus, as recorded in Revelation 5:11 NIV, there were "ten thousand times ten thousand," which, taken literally, would be 100 million angels. So it's not so surprising that the shepherds' immediate response to their announcement was to head off to Bethlehem, saying, "Let's go." No one had to form a committee to consider it.

At Christmas, angels fulfilled one of their most prominent purposes: to deliver God's messages. Divine airmail. The very word *angel* means messenger. Not only did they make the ultimate birth announcement, but God sent the angel Gabriel and an angel of the Lord to Mary (Luke 1) and Joseph (Matt. 1:20–21) to tell the parents beforehand about their special Son.

The baby in that manger was not the only baby that angels watch over, however. Jesus said, "See to it that you don't despise one of these little ones, because I tell you that in heaven their angels continually view the face of my Father in heaven" (Matt. 18:10). By implication and in context of the passage, the Father in heaven is very concerned about every child and ready to deploy His angels rather than let one be turned away from the gospel by the discouragement of being despised.

There's no doubt that angels play a big part in the execution of God's rescue plans—corporate and individual. Angels are all over the Christmas scene, appropriately, since they delivered the save-the-date announcement and an army of them formed the first Christmas parade. But this Christmas, you can get to know a pair of angels who once had a front-row seat, the very best view of God's Christmas gift of *mercy*.

The plan for the first Christmas was made centuries before the big day. God, in His infinite wisdom and perfect timing, revealed His rescue plan for humanity in various ways at various times throughout the history of the Old Testament (Luke 24:15–27). In one spectacularly detailed example, God arranged for the center of worship, the tabernacle and later the temple, to preview the gospel. Inside the tabernacle, in the Holy of Holies, stood the Ark of the Covenant. Among the detailed instructions for the tabernacle that the Lord gave Moses were instructions for this Ark, a chest about 4 feet by 2½ feet and 2½ feet high, made of acacia wood. It had gold rings at each corner for poles to slide through to carry the box. Here is what the ark contained:

- **The Ten Commandments** (Exod. 20:1–17)
- **Manna** – A golden urn containing manna from heaven. The manna was God's provision for His people when they complained and groused, having just been rescued from slavery (Exod. 16:1–4).

- **Moses's brother Aaron's budding rod** – The rod that God chose to spontaneously cause to bud, producing almonds and blossoms, and put an end to the tribes' rebellion against God's authority and appointment of the Levite tribe as the priests for the community. It was to serve as a warning against any further rebellion (Num. 17).

The Ark contained God's law, God's powerful (even eatable) grace, and a symbol of God's mighty mercy in light of humanity's rebellion (Heb. 9:4–5).

The Ark also had a lid, a very important lid, a cover for the box made of pure gold. At each end of the lid was a cherub made of hammered gold. The pair of golden cherubim, a very particular type of angel, were to be attached to the lid. Their wings spread upward, overshadowing the lid or cover, and they faced each other but looked *toward* the golden lid (Exod. 25:10–22 NLT).

Above those cherubim, over the ark of the covenant, God Himself would meet with Moses. It was His throne on Earth.

> *22 There, **above the cover between the two cherubim that are over the ark of the covenant law, I will meet with you** and give you all my commands for the Israelites* (Exod. 25:22 NIV, emphasis added).

> *LORD Almighty, the God of Israel, **enthroned between the cherubim**, you alone are God over all the kingdoms of the earth. You have made heaven and earth* (Isa. 37:16 NIV, emphasis added).

> *The LORD reigns, let the nations tremble; **he sits enthroned between the cherubim**, let the earth shake* (Ps. 99:1NIV, emphasis added).

As spectacular as God's presence is, the lid is worth notice. Above the law and below the Lord God Almighty was the lid. The lid of the ark. The lid made of gold. The lid that covered the law. The lid that covered the reminders of man's faithless complaining and rebellion and God's abundant grace and mercy. The lid that was guarded over by the representative watchful eyes of two golden cherubim. That lid was the **mercy seat.**

Underneath the mercy seat was the law. The law that no one kept. The law by which we're all condemned (Gal. 3:11–12). And, in light of the law-breaking nature of all humankind, no human could come into the presence of a holy, perfect God. Yet *above* the mercy seat was the very presence of the living God. How? The root word translated *mercy seat* is the same as that for *atonement.* More literally, in the Greek, it is called the *hilasterion* or propitiation seat. Effectively, the **covering** seat or the atonement lid.[1]

73

It was on that lid that the blood of animals sacrificed to pay for the sins of the people was sprinkled (Lev. 16:11–15). That lid. That cover. That atonement. The barrier between God's presence and the broken law. The cover over all the law that we can't keep on our own. The precious gold that protected those seated in mercy. It's no wonder that the two golden cherubim were to be made with eyes fixed on that mercy seat.

Just as it was at the first Christmas, where the army of angels' attention and worship were fixed on the ultimate messenger of mercy, the cherubim were fixated on the mercy seat. The cherubim were pointed toward the mercy seat that would, at Christmas, be replaced permanently with our Savior.

> [25] *God presented **Christ as a sacrifice of atonement**, through the shedding of his blood—to be received by faith. He did this to demonstrate his righteousness, because in his forbearance he had left the sins committed beforehand unpunished—* [26] *he did it to demonstrate his righteousness at the present time, so as to be just and the one who justifies those who have faith in Jesus* (Rom. 3:25–26 NIV, emphasis added).

Jesus was the *hilasterion*. He was the propitiation—the **cover** that protects us from the wrath we deserve for breaking the law, God's law of perfect love, perfect justice, perfect holiness. Jesus was and is the **Mercy Seat**.

The two cherubim were symbolically doing the job they had done at the fall of humankind: guarding the threshold between sinners and a holy God. At the fall of humankind, God kicked Adam and Eve out of the garden. While it may not be readily apparent, that act, in part, was an act of mercy. Had they remained in the garden, they would be doomed to live forever in their sinful, fallen state. Doomed to live out the consequences of sin eternally. The prospect that they would live mortally, where their lives on Earth in their fallen, broken, hurting, cursed, painful state would at some point come to an end and they would then have a chance to be resurrected and redeemed to rejoin the Lord once again, was **mercy**. So the Lord placed the cherubim as guards outside the garden: "After he drove the man out, he placed on the east side of the Garden of Eden cherubim and a flaming sword flashing back and forth to guard the way to the tree of life" (Gen. 3:24 NIV). On the one hand, they were guards to the unapproachable holy garden.[2] But on the other hand, they were keeping humankind from living eternally cursed. They were witnesses to God's mercy.

In the tabernacle, images of cherubim were likewise woven into the texture of the curtains and the inner veil that separated the Holy of Holies from the remainder of the tent (Exod. 26:1, 31–33). They would represent His holy presence. Exposure to that holy presence of God, *without the mercy seat*, would mean instant death (Exod. 33:20,

Rom. 3:23). The golden angels were yet again witnesses to mercy—a holy God meeting with His inherently sinful people, withholding His wrath, allowing them to live by the merciful provision of blood sacrifices and the protection of the mercy seat.

In Christ, we have the embodiment of mercy. Read the Lord's sumptuous invitation to feast upon His mercy found in our Mercy Seat:

> *¹ Come, all you who are thirsty, come to the waters; and you who have no money, come, buy and eat! Come, buy wine and milk without money and without cost. ² Why spend money on what is not bread, and your labor on what does not satisfy? Listen, listen to me, and eat what is good, and you will delight in the richest of fare. ³ Give ear and come to me; listen, that you may live. I will make an everlasting covenant with you, my faithful love promised to David* (Isa. 55:1–3 NIV).

The Lord calls us in for dinner to feast on what's eternal and what satisfies, what money cannot buy but with which riches cannot compare—the covenant of grace that was paid for by the blood of Christ. The promise of our salvation.

> *⁶ Seek the LORD while he may be found; call on him while he is near. ⁷ Let the wicked forsake their ways and the unrighteous their thoughts. Let them turn to the LORD, and he will have mercy on them, and to our God, for he will freely pardon. ⁸ "For my thoughts are not your thoughts, neither are your ways my ways," declares the LORD. ⁹ "As the heavens are higher than the earth, so are my ways higher than your ways and my thoughts than your thoughts"* (Isa. 55:6–9).

God doesn't call the cleaned-up to the table. He calls the wicked and the unrighteous. He invites them to turn to Him and offers them mercy and a *free* pardon. Why? Because He is *not like* us. He's not like any one of us. He's not like the merciless people around us. He's not more interested in being right than being in a relationship. He's more interested in our praise than penalty and payment. He's more interested in our freedom than in imposing a life sentence.

> *¹⁰ As the rain and the snow come down from heaven, and do not return to it without watering the earth and making it bud and flourish, so that it yields seed for the sower and bread for the eater, ¹¹ so is my word that goes out from my mouth: It will not return to me empty, but will accomplish what I desire and achieve the purpose for which I sent it. ¹² You will go out in joy and be led forth in peace; the mountains and hills will burst into song before you, and all the trees of the field will clap their hands. ¹³ Instead of the thornbush will grow the juniper, and instead of briers the myrtle will grow. This will be for the LORD's renown, for an everlasting sign, that will endure forever"* (Isa. 55:10–13).

His mercy results in holding back the scorched-earth treatment we deserve in favor of the fertile filling of His purposeful Word. His mercy and grace make an impact on us not just for today, but for eternity.

When we experience compassion, it's from our Father. "Blessed be the God and Father of our Lord Jesus Christ, the Father of mercies and the God of all comfort" (2 Cor. 1:3). When we are able to persevere, it's because of His mercy. "See, we count as blessed those who have endured. You have heard of Job's endurance and have seen the outcome that the Lord brought about—the Lord is compassionate and merciful" (James 5:11). When we lack clear identity and then come to know we're His, that's His mercy. "Once you were not a people, but now you are God's people; you had not received mercy, but now you have received mercy" (1 Pet. 2:10). When we're unexpectedly healed or rescued from pain, that's His mercy (Mark 5:19, Phil. 2:27). When our past is not as loud as our present hope, that's His mercy (Luke 18:13, 1 Tim. 1:13).

When *we* are merciful, it is because *He* was merciful first (Luke 6:36). And it is only in view of His mercy that we can freely give our life as a living sacrifice in worship to the God who saved it in the first place (Rom. 12:1). If we'd gotten what we deserve, we'd be dust with no life to give.

As God sits on the head of Satan, our accuser, keeping a *lid* on him and what he has to say, we can come before His throne and worship our merciful, compassionate God, looking forward in hope to the time we will rejoin Him. In the meantime, "Because of the LORD's faithful love we do not perish, for his mercies never end. They are new every morning; great is your faithfulness!" (Lam. 3:22–23). As you approach His throne in prayer during this Christmas season and beyond, you might wave to the cherubim standing in guardian stance. Your access beyond their wings and your refuge beneath them was paid for by God's generous gifts of mercy and grace.

MERCY:
GIFT #7 SUMMARY AND SCRIPTURES

SUMMARY

Angels have served, and continue to serve, in many roles in the service of the Lord. The angels who announced Christ's coming and arrival were announcing much more than a birth—they were announcing the execution of God's eternal rescue plan. As we ponder the enormity of His plan to make a way to rejoin and reconcile with humanity, it would be hard to miss His rich gift of mercy. A vivid picture of His mercy can be found in the mercy seat, the lid on the ark of the covenant. Jesus is the new mercy seat, the covering that protects us from the righteous wrath of God that we deserve. He stood in the middle between our lawbreaking, complaint-making, rebellious hearts and God's perfect holiness, and He laid down His life on the altar, covering our lives with His holiness. From the cherubim's witness of God's mercy during the fall of humankind and tabernacle worship, to the Christmas announcement of His mercy mission, the angels haven't missed a beat. We can wake every morning to the invitation to join them in praising God for the new mercies He offers us every day.

SCRIPTURES FOR GIFT #7

Luke 2:8–20

⁸ In the same region, shepherds were staying out in the fields and keeping watch at night over their flock. ⁹ Then an angel of the Lord stood before them, and the glory of the Lord shone around them, and they were terrified. ¹⁰ But the angel said to them, "Don't be afraid, for look, I proclaim to you good news of great joy that will be for all the people: ¹¹ Today in the city of David a Savior was born for you, who is the Messiah, the Lord. ¹² This will be the sign for you: You will find a baby wrapped tightly in cloth and lying in a manger."

¹³ Suddenly there was a multitude of the heavenly host with the angel, praising God and saying:

¹⁴ Glory to God in the highest heaven,

and peace on earth to people he favors!

¹⁵ When the angels had left them and returned to heaven, the shepherds said to one another, "Let's go straight to Bethlehem and see what has happened, which the Lord has made known to us."

¹⁶ They hurried off and found both Mary and Joseph, and the baby who was lying in the manger. ¹⁷ After seeing them, they reported the message they were told about this child, ¹⁸ and all who heard it were amazed at what the shepherds said to them. ¹⁹ But Mary was treasuring up all these things in her heart and meditating on them.

²⁰ The shepherds returned, glorifying and praising God for all the things they had seen and heard, which were just as they had been told.

Revelation 5:11 NIV

¹¹ Then I looked and heard the voice of many angels, numbering thousands upon thousands, and ten thousand times ten thousand. They encircled the throne and the living creatures and the elders.

Matthew 18:10

¹⁰ See to it that you don't despise one of these little ones, because I tell you that in heaven their angels continually view the face of my Father in heaven.

Hebrews 9:3–5

³ Behind the second curtain was a tent called the most holy place. ⁴ It had the gold altar of incense and the ark of the covenant, covered with gold on all sides, in which was a gold jar containing the manna, Aaron's staff that budded, and the tablets of the covenant. ⁵ The cherubim of glory were above the ark overshadowing the mercy seat. It is not possible to speak about these things in detail right now.

Exodus 25:22 NIV

²² There, **above the cover between the two cherubim that are over the ark of the covenant law, I will meet with you** and give you all my commands for the Israelites (emphasis added).

Isaiah 37:16 NIV

¹⁶ Lord Almighty, the God of Israel, **enthroned between the cherubim**, You alone are God over all the kingdoms of the earth You have made heaven and earth (emphasis added).

Psalm 99:1 NIV

¹ The Lord reigns, let the nations tremble; **he sits enthroned between the cherubim**, let the earth shake (emphasis added).

Leviticus 16:11–15

¹¹ "When Aaron presents the bull for his sin offering and makes atonement for himself and his household, he will slaughter the bull for his sin offering. ¹² Then he is to take a firepan full of blazing coals from the altar before the Lord and two handfuls of finely ground fragrant incense, and bring them inside the curtain. ¹³ He is to put the incense on the fire before the Lord, so that the cloud of incense covers the mercy seat that is over the testimony, or else he will die. ¹⁴ He is to take some

of the bull's blood and sprinkle it with his finger against the east side of the mercy seat; then he will sprinkle some of the blood with his finger before the mercy seat seven times.

¹⁵ "When he slaughters the male goat for the people's sin offering and brings its blood inside the curtain, he will do the same with its blood as he did with the bull's blood: He is to sprinkle it against the mercy seat and in front of it."

Romans 3:25–26 NIV

²⁵ God presented Christ as a sacrifice of **atonement**, through the shedding of his blood—to be received by faith. He did this to demonstrate his righteousness, because in his forbearance he had left the sins committed beforehand unpunished— ²⁶ he did it to demonstrate his righteousness at the present time, so as to be just and the one who justifies those who have faith in Jesus (emphasis added).

Genesis 3:24 NIV

²⁴ After he drove the man out, he placed on the east side of the Garden of Eden cherubim and a flaming sword flashing back and forth to guard the way to the tree of life.

Exodus 26:1, 31–33

¹You are to construct the tabernacle itself with ten curtains. You must make them of finely spun linen, and blue, purple, and scarlet yarn, with a design of cherubim worked into them.

³¹ You are to make a curtain of blue, purple, and scarlet yarn, and finely spun linen with a design of cherubim worked into it. ³² Hang it on four gold-plated pillars of acacia wood that have gold hooks and that stand on four silver bases. ³³ Hang the curtain under the clasps and bring the ark of the testimony there behind the curtain, so the curtain will make a separation for you between the holy place and the most holy place.

Exodus 33:20 NIV

²⁰ "But," he said, "you cannot see my face, for no one may see me and live."

Romans 3:23

²³ For all have sinned and fall short of the glory of God.

Isaiah 55:1–3, 6–13

¹ "Come, everyone who is thirsty, come to the water; and you without silver, come, buy, and eat! Come, buy wine and milk without silver and without cost! ² Why do you spend silver on what is not food, and your wages on what does not satisfy? Listen carefully to me, and eat what is good, and you will enjoy the choicest of foods. ³ Pay

attention and come to me; listen, so that you will live. I will make a permanent covenant with you on the basis of the faithful kindnesses of David.

[6] Seek the LORD while he may be found; call to him while he is near. [7] Let the wicked one abandon his way and the sinful one his thoughts; let him return to the LORD, so he may have compassion on him, and to our God, for he will freely forgive. [8] "For my thoughts are not your thoughts, and your ways are not my ways." This is the LORD's declaration. [9] "For as heaven is higher than earth, so my ways are higher than your ways, and my thoughts than your thoughts.

[10] For just as rain and snow fall from heaven and do not return there without saturating the earth and making it germinate and sprout, and providing seed to sow and food to eat, [11] so my word that comes from my mouth will not return to me empty, but it will accomplish what I please and will prosper in what I send it to do. [12] You will indeed go out with joy and be peacefully guided; the mountains and the hills will break into singing before you, and all the trees of the field will clap their hands. [13] Instead of the thornbush, a cypress will come up, and instead of the brier, a myrtle will come up; this will stand as a monument for the Lord, an everlasting sign that will not be destroyed."

2 Corinthians 1:3

[3] Blessed be the God and Father of our Lord Jesus Christ, the Father of mercies and the God of all comfort.

James 5:11

[11] See, we count as blessed those who have endured. You have heard of Job's endurance and have seen the outcome that the Lord brought about—the Lord is compassionate and merciful.

1 Peter 2:10

[10] Once you were not a people, but now you are God's people; you had not received mercy, but now you have received mercy.

Mark 5:18–19

[18] As he was getting into the boat, the man who had been demon-possessed begged him earnestly that he might remain with him. [19] Jesus did not let him but told him, "Go home to your own people, and report to them how much the Lord has done for you and how he has had mercy on you."

Philippians 2:27

[27] Indeed, he was so sick that he nearly died. However, God had mercy on him, and not only on him but also on me, so that I would not have sorrow upon sorrow.

Luke 18:13

¹³ "But the tax collector, standing far off, would not even raise his eyes to heaven but kept striking his chest and saying, 'God, have mercy on me, a sinner!'"

1 Timothy 1:13 NIV

¹³ Even though I was once a blasphemer and a persecutor and a violent man, I was shown mercy because I acted in ignorance and unbelief.

Luke 6:36

³⁶ Be merciful, just as your Father also is merciful.

Romans 12:1 NIV

¹ Therefore, I urge you, brothers and sisters, in view of God's mercy, to offer your bodies as a living sacrifice, holy and pleasing to God—this is your true and proper worship.

Lamentations 3:22–23

²² Because of the Lord's faithful love we do not perish, for his mercies never end. ²³ They are new every morning; great is your faithfulness!

MERCY:
GIFT #7 REFLECTION AND PRAYER

REFLECTION QUESTIONS

1. The French word for saying "thank you," *merci*, is from the same base word for mercy. We may often say thanks for what we receive, but how often do you find yourself giving thanks for mercy—*not* getting what you actually deserved? Take a moment to thank the Lord for the consequences deserved but not delivered.

2. Romans 12:1 calls for us to be a living sacrifice as our form of worship. That's a tough standard. Total surrender. Putting your plans, priorities, and philosophies on the altar and giving Him precedence. How does His mercy make it easier or harder to be a living sacrifice? What about His mercy changes the nature and difficulty of this command? Where would our plans, priorities, and philosophies be if he were *not* merciful?

3. Who needs your mercy this Christmas? How about *everyone*! Think about gifts of mercy you might give this year. What mistakes might you overlook? What inconsiderate offenses could you love people through?

4. God's Word says that His mercies are new *every day* (Lam. 3:22–23). Make a list of the mercies you received today. What consequences did you deserve today that you dodged? What circumstances did He pull you out of that you couldn't earn your way out of? Pick a day or two this week to identify God's constant acts of mercy on your behalf.

PRAYER

Merciful Father God, thank you for reminding me of Your covering, that You provided Your own Son as a shield between my sin and Your righteous judgment. Like Your angels, let me freely bear witness to Your holiness and the mercy You've so generously given. You spared me the wages of death—what I deserve—and instead gave me the riches of your grace by making Christ pay my wage and give over the riches of His inheritance. Not only are you compassionate, and not only does your compassion never fail, but you are the Father of compassion, its originator and creator. When I persevere, when I claim my identity as your child, when I'm a vessel of mercy, it's because of *Your* mercy and grace. Thank you that my past pain is in the shadow of my present hope because I hide in the refuge of Your mercy. Amen.

GIFT #8: PROTECTION

Mark 11:9–10, Matthew 2:1–12, Psalm. 136:3, Isaiah 53:4–6,
Romans 4:24–25, Psalm 23:1–5, Philippians 4:6–7, Proverbs 3:5–6,
Psalm 119:105, Ephesians 6:12, 1 John 2:15–17, 1 Corinthians 15:26,
Philippians 3:20–21, 2 Corinthians 4:16–17, Proverbs 16:7,
1 Peter 5:10, Colossians 3:2–4, John 10:28–29, Psalm 25:20

Peppermint is a hybrid between water mint and spearmint and has been associated with all kinds of health benefits, from helping with coughs and colds to freshening breath and improving memory and alertness. Students might pop a peppermint candy on test-taking day to stay on the ball.[1] But at Christmas, when it's mixed into candy and shaped into candy cane sticks and candy cane staffs, it carries with it a sweet but powerful symbol of our Protector.

This Christmas, as you enjoy candy canes,
stuff them into stockings, or decorate the tree with them,
let them remind you of a rod and staff,
the tools of our God, the tools of our Protector.

At Christmas, we celebrate the earthly arrival of the King. When He arrived on Earth, many Jewish people were awaiting a king, but one that would be an earthly ruler with the distinctive feature that he was sent by God. Their chief hope was that this king, the messiah or savior, would free them from vicious, horrific Roman oppression and restore the nation of Israel to its former glory by crushing the enemy and wiping out those who were unfaithful to God. When Jesus rode into Jerusalem for the last Passover He'd have before His crucifixion, he received an anointed king's welcome.

⁹ Those who went ahead and those who followed shouted:

> *Hosanna!*
>
> **Blessed is he who comes in the name of the Lord!**
>
> ¹⁰ Blessed is the coming kingdom of our father David!
>
> *Hosanna* in the highest heaven! (Mark 11:9–10).

They were excitedly hoping for a my-god-beats-your-god showdown like the one Elijah got to participate in (1 Kings 18:21).

We can relate to that hope today. We all might look to a change of leadership or a battle-tested tough guy to rescue us from significant problems and protect us from our enemies. It is no coincidence that superhero movies, where the hero beats down the bad guys, sell big. And faithful followers of the Lord do rightly desire and pray to the Lord to fight their battles (Exod. 14:14).

Jesus did come as king—the King of Kings, in fact (Ps. 136:3, Deut. 10:17, Rev. 1:5, 17:14, 19:11–16). The wise men visited Jesus when He was likely around two years old, acknowledging He was the King and was born just where the Messianic King was supposed to be (Matt. 2:1–12, Mic. 5:1–2). Jesus also spoke of and taught on the Kingdom of God more than any other subject.

But the Savior who arrived on Earth at Jesus's birth was far more than your average king or tough guy. He came as a humble king. He came to save, not by the blood of enemies, but by His own blood. Not by grandeur, but by grace. Not by vengeance, but by forgiveness. Not as a tough guy, but as a sacrifice. And He had another job title that came as a Christmas surprise: Shepherd. He is the Shepherd of shepherds. His birth announcement by a host of angels **went to a bunch of shepherds first**, almost as if to signal that He'd come with a shepherd's status and a shepherd's heart. But shepherds at that time were the lowest men on the social totem pole. They were looked down on and considered almost unclean. Moses's demotion from prince in Pharaoh's house to shepherd of a flock would have been a cataclysmic drop in social status, but God's chosen people were not all prepared for their Messiah to take the same job and status adjustment.

The Shepherd came to care for and protect His sheep. God compares us all to sheep, and Isaiah describes how our Savior, the Lord's arm, a tender shoot, while held in low esteem just like a lowly shepherd, came to Earth to rescue His sheep.

> *¹ Who has believed our message and to whom has the arm of the LORD been revealed?*
>
> *² He grew up before him like a tender shoot, and like a root out of dry ground.*
>
> *He had no beauty or majesty to attract us to him, nothing in his appearance that we should desire him.*

*³ He was despised and rejected by mankind, a man of suffering, and familiar with pain. Like one from whom people hide their faces he was despised, and **we held him in low esteem**.*

⁴ Surely he took up our pain and bore our suffering, yet we considered him punished by God, stricken by him, and afflicted.

⁵ But he was pierced for our transgressions, he was crushed for our iniquities; the punishment that brought us peace was on him, and by his wounds we are healed.

*⁶ We all, **like sheep, have gone astray**, each of us has turned to our own way; and the LORD has laid on him the iniquity of us all* (Isa. 53:1–6 NIV, emphasis added) (see also John 10:14).

Not only did he take upon Himself all our iniquity, all our sin, all our mistakes, shortcomings, and the wrongs we would do in our lifetime—but he died the death of a sheep so His sheep could live forever.

*⁷ He was oppressed and afflicted, yet he did not open his mouth; he was **led like a lamb to the slaughter, and as a sheep before its shearers is silent**, so he did not open his mouth. ⁸ By oppression and judgment he was taken away. Yet who of his generation protested? For he was cut off from the land of the living; for the transgression of my people he was punished* (Isa. 53:7–8 NIV, emphasis added).

²⁴ [B]ut also for us, to whom God will credit righteousness—for us who believe in him who raised Jesus our Lord from the dead. ²⁵ He was delivered over to death for our sins and was raised to life for our justification (Rom. 4:24–25 NIV).

Can you imagine leading a flock of sheep? Sheep that hurt themselves? Sheep that are constantly going astray, wandering off, and needing care? Now imagine you were in a situation where it's you—or the sheep. Either you take a dive off a cliff, or they do. Either you go to the slaughter, or they will. We might all be tempted to let the fluffy guys go, given that decision. But that's not the Shepherd we have. He cares for us so much that He was willing to die for us. First and foremost, Jesus **protected us** from the righteous wrath of God. He protected us from the judgment we deserve and took it upon Himself so we could go home and graze with God forever.

But as a flock, we're not home yet. For this world is not our permanent home; we are looking forward to a home yet to come (Heb. 13:14 NLT). And not only is Jesus the kind of shepherd willing to go to the slaughter in place of the herd, He is the kind of shepherd who protects us *through* the dangers of this world to get us home.

As we experience the suffering our fallen world and ways deliver, sometimes even at the hands of those supposed to protect and lead us, it's easy to let our trust in God's gift of protection be shaken. But His protection through the hurts and deep brokenness of this world is far deeper and greater than we might imagine. Although His role as our shepherd involves providing for our needs, both physical and spiritual (Ps. 23:2–3), His loving guidance actually protects us along the path and helps heal our wounds.

When David, a shepherd himself, described the Lord as his shepherd, he understood that sheep as a livestock class are very high maintenance.[2] Sheep would get skittish with fast-moving waters, so a good shepherd would lead his sheep beside *still* waters. We can trust Jesus to free us from anxiety by protecting our hearts so we can get a tall drink of spiritual refreshment without worry. We need only bring our requests to Him expectantly, ready to thank Him for His continued faithfulness through the hardships and hurts, and He will supernaturally guard our hearts from fear (Phil. 4:6–7).

David also knew that sheep had to be guided down the *right* paths because there were a lot of wrong ones that would put the sheep in danger. He knew that the Lord protects us by making our paths straight (not letting us wander down sketchy cliffs), if only we'll acknowledge Him in all that we do. If only we will look up and see that the Shepherd's got a flashlight and a staff to show us the way, He'll keep us on the righteous path (Ps 23:3–4, Prov. 3:5–6, Ps. 119:105). In case we forget, His staff bears the shape of His initial (at least in English)—it looks like a *J* turned upside down.

But then, you might still be craving the tough guy, the big brother who stands up for you, the guardian who fights your battles. Our Shepherd is that, too. The real battle we fight, the one that seeks to threaten our forever-life and not just this short one, is a battle for the mind and heart, one fought by powers outmatched only by our Shepherd (Eph. 6:12, 1 John 2:15–17). Put another way, with obedience to and covering of the divine power and might of our Shepherd, we demolish the plans and schemes of the enemy, the father of lies—Satan himself. "For though we live in the world, we do not wage war as the world does. The weapons we fight with are not the weapons of the world. On the contrary, they have divine power to demolish strongholds. We demolish arguments and every pretension that sets itself up against the knowledge of God, and we take captive every thought to make it obedient to Christ" (2 Cor. 10:3–5 NIV). We will even defeat the last enemy, death, by living forever in resurrected, renewed, glorified bodies (1 Cor. 15:26, Phil. 3:20–21, 2 Cor. 4:16–17). And as we walk in faith and obedience to our Shepherd, He will make even our enemies live at peace with us, preparing a table for us right in front of them (Prov. 16:7, Ps. 23:5).

Not only does Jesus carry His staff to guide us but also the rod to beat the snot out of the enemy of our souls and those who seek to threaten our promised everlasting life with Him (Ps. 23:4).

God also cares for our needs. When we stack up battle scars, His love binds our wounds and soothes them with the oil of His anointing (Ps 147:3, Ps. 23:5). He will personally attend to them. "The God of all grace, who called you to his eternal glory in Christ, will himself restore, establish, strengthen, and support you after you have suffered a little while" (1 Pet. 5:10).

For the ultimate protection of your eternal life, He has hidden life in Himself. He has your forever-life, the ending to your story, hidden in His person so no one and nothing can do it harm (Col. 3:2–4, John 10:28–29). In the very end, the end that never ends, Jesus will be our King of glory—ushering in the new heaven and new Earth for eternity. "And when the Chief Shepherd appears, you will receive the crown of glory that does not fade away" (1 Pet. 5:4 NIV).

In this Christmas season, you may be wounded and weary, you may be celebrating a good year, but your Shepherd is keenly aware of your every step and seeks to protect the forever-life you've been given and guide you safely home through the darkness of this world. Enjoy the sweetness of peppermint candy (or use it in a decoration for a sugar-free option), and let it remind you of the Shepherd's staff to guide you and the Shepherd's rod to beat off the enemy along the way as you stay in the shelter of His protection (Ps. 25:20).

PROTECTION:
GIFT #8 SUMMARY AND SCRIPTURE

SUMMARY

At Christmas, while we may see Jesus as a distant King, He is not only the King of Kings but, in fact, a close-by Shepherd. He left the safety of His home in heaven to enter the dangers of this world so He could die on behalf of His sheep. His protection extends to supernatural protection of our hearts and a willingness to lead us down straight paths if we'll follow His flashlight-lit direction. He'll fight alongside us with His divine power against the enemy and guard our forever-life in His very hand. And He binds up our wounds, restoring us to the eternal glory of the home He calls us to. We need only trust the purpose of our lives in His hands. The sweet candy cane staff and rod can be a reminder of the sweet grace of our Shepherd as he gives us the gifts of guidance and protection.

SCRIPTURES FOR GIFT #8

Mark 11:9–10

[9] Those who went ahead and those who followed shouted:

Hosanna!

Blessed is he who comes in the name of the Lord!

[10] Blessed is the coming kingdom of our father David!

Hosanna in the highest heaven!

Matthew 2:1–12 NLT

[1] Jesus was born in Bethlehem in Judea, during the reign of King Herod. About that time some wise men from eastern lands arrived in Jerusalem, asking, [2] **"Where is the newborn king of the Jews? We saw his star as it rose, and we have come to worship him."**

[3] King Herod was deeply disturbed when he heard this, as was everyone in Jerusalem. [4] He called a meeting of the leading priests and teachers of religious law and asked, "Where is the Messiah supposed to be born?"

[5] "In Bethlehem in Judea," they said, "for this is what the prophet wrote:

[6] 'And you, O Bethlehem in the land of Judah,

are not least among the ruling cities of Judah,

for a ruler will come from you

who will be the shepherd for my people Israel.'"

[7] Then Herod called for a private meeting with the wise men, and he learned from them the time when the star first appeared. [8] Then he told them, "Go to Bethlehem and search carefully for the child. And when you find him, come back and tell me so that I can go and worship him, too!"

⁹ After this interview the wise men went their way. And the star they had seen in the east guided them to Bethlehem. It went ahead of them and stopped over the place where the child was. ¹⁰ When they saw the star, they were filled with joy! ¹¹ They entered the house and saw the child with his mother, Mary, and they bowed down and worshiped him. Then they opened their treasure chests and gave him gifts of gold, frankincense, and myrrh.

¹² When it was time to leave, they returned to their own country by another route, for God had warned them in a dream not to return to Herod (emphasis added).

Psalm 136:3

³ Give thanks to the Lord of lords: His faithful love endures forever.

Isaiah 53:4–6 NIV

⁴ Surely he took up our pain and bore our suffering, yet we considered him punished by God, stricken by him, and afflicted. ⁵ But he was pierced for our transgressions, he was crushed for our iniquities; the punishment that brought us peace was on him, and by his wounds we are healed.

⁶ We all, **like sheep, have gone astray**, each of us has turned to our own way; and the Lord has laid on him the iniquity of us all (emphasis added).

Romans 4:24–25 NIV

²⁴ [B]ut also for us, to whom God will credit righteousness—for us who believe in him who raised Jesus our Lord from the dead. ²⁵ He was delivered over to death for our sins and was raised to life for our justification.

Psalm 23

¹ The Lord is my shepherd; I have what I need. ² He lets me lie down in green pastures; he leads me beside quiet waters. ³ He renews my life; he leads me along the right paths for his name's sake.

⁴ Even when I go through the darkest valley, I fear no danger, for you are with me; your rod and your staff—they comfort me. ⁵ You prepare a table before me in the presence of my enemies; you anoint my head with oil; my cup overflows. ⁶ Only goodness and faithful love will pursue me all the days of my life, and I will dwell in the house of the Lord as long as I live.

Philippians 4:6–7

⁶ Don't worry about anything, but in everything, through prayer and petition with thanksgiving, present your requests to God. ⁷ And the peace of God, which surpasses all understanding, will guard your hearts and minds in Christ Jesus.

Proverbs 3:5–6 NIV

[5] Trust in the L<small>ORD</small> with all your heart and lean not on your own understanding; [6] in all your ways submit to him, and he will make your paths straight.

Psalm 119:105

[105] Your word is a lamp for my feet and a light on my path.

Ephesians 6:12 NIV

[12] For our struggle is not against flesh and blood, but against the rulers, against the authorities, against the powers of this dark world and against the spiritual forces of evil in the heavenly realms.

1 John 2:16–17

[16] For everything in the world—the lust of the flesh, the lust of the eyes, and the pride in one's possessions—is not from the Father, but is from the world. [17] And the world with its lust is passing away, but the one who does the will of God remains. forever.

1 Corinthians 15:26 NIV

[26] The last enemy to be destroyed in death.

Philippians 3:20–21

[20] [B]ut our citizenship is in heaven, and we eagerly wait for a Savior from there, the Lord Jesus Christ. [21] He will transform the body of our humble condition into the likeness of his glorious body, by the power that enables him to subject everything to himself.

2 Corinthians 4:16–17

[16] Therefore we do not give up. Even though our outer person is being destroyed, our inner person is being renewed day by day. [17] For our momentary light affliction is producing for us an absolutely incomparable eternal weight of glory.

Proverbs 16:7

[7] When a person's ways please the L<small>ORD</small>, he makes even his enemies to be at peace with him.

1 Peter 5:10 NIV

[10] And the God of all grace, who called you to his eternal glory in Christ, after you have suffered a little while, will himself restore you and make you strong, firm and steadfast.

Colossians 3:2–4

² Set your minds on things above, not on earthly things. ³ For you died, and your life is hidden with Christ in God. ⁴ When Christ, who is your life, appears, then you also will appear with him in glory.

John 10:28–29

²⁸ I give them eternal life, and they will never perish. No one will snatch them out of my hand. ²⁹ My Father, who has given them to me, is greater than all. No one is able to snatch them out of the Father's hand.

1 Peter 5:4 NIV

⁴ And when the Chief Shepherd appears, you will receive the crown of glory that does not fade away.

Psalm 25:20 NIV

²⁰ Guard my life and rescue me; do not let me be put to shame, for I take refuge in you

PROTECTION:
GIFT #8 REFLECTION AND PRAYER

REFLECTION QUESTIONS

1. Do you view Jesus more as a distant ruler or a watchful shepherd? How does it change your day-to-day comings and goings if He is intimately interested in guiding and protecting you? How does Proverbs 3:5–6 suggest we might miss out on the blessings or benefit from His shepherding?

2. To protect us from all sin, God would have to put all sinners to death. According to Isaiah 53:6, who does that include? Our perfectly loving Father God waits patiently for humankind to take Him up on His rescue plan and place their faith in the perfect sacrifice He sent, the only sacrifice that was perfectly pure, fully man, and fully God. When we put our trust in Him, Jesus serves as a substitute for humankind and takes on the righteous, just wrath of our perfectly just God. Only with justice paid could a perfectly pure and holy God commune with sinful, fallen humans. How does knowing the character of God (perfectly loving, perfectly just, and perfectly holy) help you *trust* Him for your protection?

3. Read 2 Corinthians 4:16–17, Ephesians 6:12, and 1 John 2:16. What's the *real need* for protection? How's your battle plan? Ask the Lord to show you how to war well and maintain peace in your soul this Christmas.

4. Jesus said, "What do you think? If someone has a hundred sheep, and one of them goes astray, won't he leave the ninety-nine on the hillside and go and search for the stray? And if he finds it, truly I tell you, he rejoices over that sheep more than over the ninety-nine that did not go astray. In the same way, it is not the will of your Father in heaven that one of these little ones perish" (Matt. 18:12–14). Maybe you've not yet decided to follow Jesus and are feeling as if, since you're not "in" with Him, He's not the Shepherd for you. Know that He is wildly interested in you. You are, in fact, the sheep He has His eye on. Take a moment to earnestly call out to Him and ask Him to be *your* Shepherd, *your* Savior, the Protector of your soul.

PRAYER

Father, when you sent your Son at Christmas, all predicted a King, but many did not understand He would be a suffering servant, identifying with and announcing His birth to the lowly shepherds of the day. Help us listen to the voice of the Shepherd so we'll know His voice as He calls and directs, remain under his direction and protection, and conform our attitude to His so our highest priorities are to love You with all we are and care for His sheep as we care for ourselves.

CHRISTMAS DAY

THE GIFT OF HOPE

In the days leading up to Christmas Day, there is so much hope. Kids hope and hope and hope that they get the toys they really want, that Santa will come, that the day they've built up in their minds (with a little help from commercials) will be all they *hope* it will be. Some of those hopes, maybe all of them, may be realized on Christmas. Not long after, though, there can be a hole in their hope. And ours.

But Christmas is about a better hope. A bigger hope. An eternal hope. A God-sized hope. You might say that Jesus's birth announcement to the shepherds was a hope announcement. So why the hole in our hope? Because no other hope except hope in God (Ps. 42:5) can fill up our soul's stocking. All other hopes are either hopes deferred that make our hearts sick (Prov. 13:12), selfish hopes that just start fights (James 4:1–3), or, worse, hopes that stubbornly seek bad ideas and destructive desires and that God finally allows us to have (Rom. 1:18–32).

If you find your hope a little too low-calorie and unsatisfying, Jesus came to invite you to a sumptuous feast of His grace. Go ahead. Come in. Sit down at the table. Jesus says, "Ask and it will be given to you; seek and you will find; knock and the door will be opened to you. For everyone who asks receives; the one who seeks finds; and to the one who knocks, the door will be opened. Which of you, if your son asks for bread, will give him a stone? Or if he asks for a fish, will give him a snake? If you, then, though you are evil, know how to give good gifts to your children, how much more will your Father in heaven give good gifts to those who ask him!" (Matt. 7:7–11 NIV).

Come on in out of the dark, and ask away.

Ask Him to be firmly planted, not shaken by the circumstances of life, fed by the Holy Spirit with a steady diet of truth and love, producing fruit that's perfectly in season—blessings to give away just when they're needed.

Ask Him for a new beginning, for a thorough cleaning of any lingering ash in your heart and life.

Ask Him for His unfettered approval. The blood of Christ has paid for it, and He offers it for free.

Ask Him for joy. Not a temporary pick-me-up (although you can ask for that, too) but a big, glorious, heartfelt joy that puts a new song in your heart and a rhythm in your step. Ask Him for a joy that can come only from your heart's deepest longing, reuniting with your heavenly Father who loves you more than you could possibly ever know. A joy that can survive the heartbreaks and hardships of this life.

Ask Him for His friendship. He is the best, most faithful friend you will ever have. He laid down His life for you and let you into His plans.

Ask Him for provision and daily bread, but don't forget to ask Him to sustain you, to help you feast on His promises, and to show you what you most need to pack for an eternal journey.

Ask Him for mercy and forgiveness, confessing where you've gone wrong and receiving the full restoration He's willing to give.

Ask Him for protection. The enemy is waging a full-scale spiritual battle for your mind and heart. Ask God to guard your heart and give you peace beyond your wildest imagination.

Ask Him for a *living* hope. A Christmas-sized, God-gifted, living hope. Then unwrap it.

> [3] *Praise be to the God and Father of our Lord Jesus Christ! In his **great mercy** he has given us **new birth** into a **living hope** through the resurrection of Jesus Christ from the dead,* [4] *and into an **inheritance** that can **never perish, spoil or fade**. This inheritance is **kept in heaven for you**,* [5] *who through faith are **shielded** by God's power until the coming of the salvation that is ready to be revealed in the last time.* [6] *In all this **you greatly rejoice**, though now for a little while you may have had to suffer grief in all kinds of trials.* [7] *These have come so that the **proven genuineness of your faith—of greater worth than gold**, which perishes even though refined by fire—may result in praise, glory and honor when Jesus Christ is revealed.* [8] *Though you have not seen him, you love him; and even though you do not see him now, **you believe in him and are filled with an inexpressible and glorious joy**,* [9] *for you are receiving the end result of your faith, the salvation of your souls* (1 Pet. 1:3–9 NIV, emphasis added).

ACKNOWLEDGMENTS

I'm especially grateful for my posse of encouragement: Rebecca Dunne, Leigh Kohler, Susannah Baker, Jean Wong, Elizabeth White-Olsen, Paula Tong, Pam Dollins, Carissa Robertson, Sherry Gremillion, and Shannon Bloodworth. You are women of mountainous faith who never hesitate to give your time, talents, and treasures to love well, to dream big dreams with me, and to act justly, love mercy, and walk humbly with God. And special thanks to Joe Parle and Don Munton for years of faithful encouragement and investment in my growth in Christ, without which I might not have had the courage to share my excitement for His Word.

NOTES

Introduction

1. "Strong's Hebrew: 4503," *BibleHub*, https://biblehub.com/hebrew/strongs_4503.htm.
2. Amy Morin, "7 Scientifically Proven Benefits of Gratitude That Will Motivate You to Give Thanks Year-Round," November 23, 2014, *Forbes*, https://www.forbes.com/sites /amymorin/2014/11/23/7-scientifically-proven-benefits-of-gratitude-that-will-motivate-you -to-give-thanks-year-round/#70c9ee89183c.

Gift #1: Firmly Planted, Fed, And Fruitful

1. "History of Christmas Trees," *History*, https://www.history.com/topics/christmas/history -of-christmas-trees.

Gift #2: New Beginnings

1. A. Noordtzij (trans. Raymond Togtman), *Leviticus: Bible Students' Commentary* (Grand Rapids, MI: Zondervan Publishing, 1982).

Gift #4: Joy

1. "Psalm" *Merriam-Webster*, https://www.merriam-webster.com/dictionary/psalm.

Gift #6: Provision

1. "Frankincense," *Oxford Reference*, http://www.oxfordreference.com/view/10.1093/oi/authority .20110803095832869.
2. "Jewish Prayers: The Blessing over Bread (HaMotzi)," *Jewish Virtual Library*, https://www .jewishvirtuallibrary.org/the-blessing-over-bread-hamotzi.
3. "Provide," *Oxford Living Dictionaries*, https://en.oxforddictionaries.com/definition/provide.

Gift #7: Mercy

1. "Hilasterion," *Bible Hub*, https://biblehub.com/greek/2435.htm.
2. "Cherubim," *Bible Study Tools*, https://www.biblestudytools.com/encyclopedias/isbe/cherubim -1.html.

Gift #8: Protection

1. Lori Aratani, "The Power of Peppermint Is Put to the Test," March 20, 2007, *Washington Post*, http://www.washingtonpost.com/wp-dyn/content/article/2007/03/19/AR2007031901624.html.

2. W. Phillip Keller, *A Shepherd Looks at Psalm 23* (Grand Rapids, MI: Zondervan Publishing, 2007), 20–21.

**For more of what you read here, please visit
www.RadiantMindz.org.**

CPSIA information can be obtained
at www.ICGtesting.com
Printed in the USA
LVHW070217201118
597629LV00018B/37/P